DYSFUNCTIONAL POLICE FAMILY

ADD INSULT TO INJURY

To Dear Ray,
'Brother in arms'.
Best Wishes.
Tom Curry.
9/11/2024.

Copyright © 2024 Tom Curry

All rights reserved.

Cover design by Tom Curry

Book design by Tom Curry

No part of this book can be reproduced in any form or by written, electronic or mechanical, including photocopying, recording, or by any information retrieval system without written permission by the author.

Published by Tom Curry Email tomwcurry@gmail.com

Although every precaution has been taken in the preparation of this book, the publisher and author assume no responsibility for errors or omissions. Neither is any liability assumed for damages resulting from the use of information contained herein.

ISBN see rear cover.

DYSFUNCTIONAL POLICE FAMILY
ADD INSULT TO INJURY

TOM CURRY

CONTENTS

CONTENTS	4
DEDICATION	6
ACKNOWLEDGEMENTS	7
FOREWORD	9
AUTHOR'S INTRODUCTION	13
CHAPTER 1 I MISS THE CIRCUS BUT NOT THE CLOWNS	16
CHAPTER 2 THE 200-YEAR-OLD SCANDAL	23
CHAPTER 3 THE FORGOTTEN INJURED	33
PC Philip Olds	33
The Bombing Outside Harrods.	35
PCs Sharon Beshenivsky and Teresa Milburn	37
PCs David Rathband	43
Angie McLoughlin	46
Martin Gill	49
Malcolm Murphy	58
Tom Curry	61
Dave Stamp	70
PC Nick Lindsay	72
Stephen Finegold	77
Pennie Payne	80

Mark Humphreys	86
Grant Prescott	90
John Smith	93
Kevin McNally	100
Andrea Brown	103
Stephen Court	107
Kay and Garry Instrell	109
John Burgess	116
Piers Lawrence	119
Lee Neale	122
Kimberley Christie-Sturges	125
Roy Saunders	131
Martin Webster	135
John Goodall	138
Clive Norman	142
Kris Aves	145
Graham Savage	149
CHAPTER 4 THE CAMPAIGN BEGINS	151
Special Police Constable Roger Gale MP	161
CHAPTER 5 THE POLICE FAMILY ADD INSULT TO INJURY	165
CHAPTER 6 THE SKULDUGGERY OF THE SUSSEX PPA	180
CHAPTER 7 THE CAMPAIGN STRUGGLE CONTINUES	195
CHAPTER 8 CONCLUSION	216

DEDICATION

To all 'fallen' and injured police officers.

ACKNOWLEDGEMENTS

Sir Roger Gale MP Kevin Moore Gordon Caldecott.

All those who contributed their story.

All who support my campaign.

The unknown originators of some photographs.

FOREWORD

I have known Tom Curry for many years, indeed ever since the mid-1980s when he was a serving Police Constable at Hastings, Sussex and I was a Detective Constable working from the same station. I formed a liking for Tom in those days due to his proactive work as a uniformed patrol officer leading to him making many arrests which he then passed on to me to further the investigation. I admired his tenacity and determination to do right by the public he served.

Roll forward a good many years and Tom became a member of the local Eastbourne & District Branch of NARPO (National Association of Retired Police Officers) of which I am the Secretary.

A couple of years ago, Tom approached me seeking some advice regarding an autobiography he was writing which he subsequently entitled, Wor Tomis the Polis. Tom is a proud Geordie and he wanted to write about his early years growing up in a number of local communities in his home county of Northumbria. He knew that since my retirement I had written and published three books relating to my previous police service. I was only too pleased to be able to assist him with advice which he readily took on board. The outcome was an extremely well written and self-published account in which he was able to articulate his undoubted wit in the appropriate places.

His book was a major success and was well received in a number of areas and Tom was rightly proud of his achievement. The book's success demonstrated to me once again, as if I needed reminding, of Tom's single-minded approach to any endeavour he undertook and his determination to produce what was an excellent product. He ruthlessly exploited social media as best as he could in an effort to boost sales and in this regard, he probably achieved more than an individual publisher could have by acting on his own behalf and initiative!

Needless to say, that following this not insignificant project, Tom quickly moved on to other things. I became aware of his campaign to secure the award of a medal to those police officers who had unfortunately been injured whilst on duty and who had then been medically retired prior to them being able to achieve the length of service required for them to receive the 'Long Service and Good Conduct Medal'.

Quite rightly, Tom identified the fact that officers themselves had been let down by the police organisation which had singularly failed to recognise their service and in many cases acts of bravery carried out by individuals leading to them sustaining the injuries which forced their retirement, and had often received no recognition whatsoever for such selfless acts.

First up, Tom attempted to garner support from prominent members of Parliament which included Sally-Ann Hart his own local MP as well as the highly popular and massively experienced MP for North Thanet in Kent, Sir Roger Gale.

In addition, Tom commenced a petition utilising change.org. However, he was advised that he should proceed through the petition process recognised by Parliament if the issue was to be addressed in the

House of Commons and receive the attention that the issue merited. Tom, with the assistance of others, set up a Facebook Group in an effort to publicise the campaign further.

It was at this point that he first spoke to me to assist him by publicising the campaign through my own Facebook Group known as Retired Officers Who Care which I was glad to do.

Subsequently, through one of the S.E. Regional NARPO NEC representatives, he had the issue raised at a full national NARPO NEC meeting where a decision was taken to fully support the campaign. NARPO currently has more than 90,000 members and one would think that such support would be a massive step forward.

However, what has happened or rather not happened to date demonstrates the apparent general lethargy towards this very worthwhile cause within the so-called Police Family.

Whilst I myself was fortunate enough to be able to complete my full police service without sustaining serious injury, I came to recognise very quickly just what an important issue this campaign covers.

As a result, I have done everything that I can to further the progress of this matter. When Tom stated that he had been approached by some members of the Facebook campaign group to write another book dealing with the issue and published this fact I gave some thought as to how I could best support him in his endeavours.

The publishing of a book about the campaign will undoubtedly assist with getting the message out there and will hopefully improve its chances of success. Without hesitation, I contacted Tom and offered to write this Foreword to his book. I felt that as a supporter of the cause who did not have a vested interest in this issue, i.e. I did not receive an injury on duty, together with the fact that I achieved senior rank, may help to add some credibility to the book.

Therefore, that is what I have now done and here it is. I hope that you the reader will enjoy Tom's book but at the same time you will understand its true meaning. I hope that you will take the time to read carefully the various first-hand accounts given by those retired police officers who have suffered an injury or injuries on duty, some really serious, which have led to their premature retirement.

Equally as important I hope that you will understand the need to ensure that their sacrifices do not go unnoticed and that they are indeed recognised for their police service with the award of an appropriate medal.

Kevin Moore BA (Hons); PgD; Retired Detective Chief Superintendent, Sussex Police

AUTHOR'S INTRODUCTION

I have written one other book, Wor Tomis The Polis (North East dialect for, Our Thomas The Policeman). This book will be nothing like the previous one, which was full of anecdotes and humour.

I said after that there would not be another from me. Seemingly, I overlooked the saying of 'Never say never'.

However, I have been persuaded to record the story of my campaign to seek proper medal recognition for severely injured police officers and the barriers I had to negotiate. Sadly, many of these have been placed by those with police connections. I was stunned to discover that many of the so-called 'police family' were reluctant to support their own unfortunate injured, even in the tiniest of ways, i.e. by even taking seconds to sign the petition.

I will also reveal that the much referenced 'police family' is nothing more than propaganda claptrap, in so much that there is no such thing in the same way that there is no supermarket staff family or any other workers' family. It sounds heartwarming and endearing but there is more evidence to contradict the statement than to support it. I much prefer to reference those in 'police circles'.

My reason for writing this book is to simply highlight the purpose of the campaign and also to dispel the absolute nonsense of there being any such thing as a 'police family' or it being even a close-knit group. To either believe or broadcast such is sheer fantasy. I will hopefully demonstrate how those officers injured whilst on duty and through no fault of their own medically retired, have been virtually cast aside with little thought having been given to the sacrifice they made.

I also wish to document the difficult campaign journey and importantly to tell the story truthfully which will help to put the record straight as to the reality of the flawed relationships within police circles and not for any other reasons.

However, I must make it perfectly clear that I do not believe the Police Service harbours any greater selfishness than any other work group does but what is different is that they are not bombarded with references to others of being members of a 'family' just because they follow the same occupation.

The book will also highlight the 200-year-old national shame in the acceptance of many police officers' sacrifices without the apparent slightest glimmer of conscience, from those who matter, of their lack of proper recognition through the award of a medal. Yes, kind words will be spoken at certain times but once that is done then normal life resumes. I question the true sincerity of many of the orators.

I am aware that what will follow may well upset certain members of the 'police family' in a similar way as Prince Harry has done with the Royal Family. At the risk of also having to flee the country, I still have the urge to tell the truth about my journey and of what I believe is a national scandal and a blot on police history going back over two centuries.

The book describes my struggle throughout the campaign. I decided on the title only after I dismissed 'Mein Kampf' when I discovered that had already been used! However, I do hope mine does as well but without me forcing all of you to buy it.

If in the unlikely event I am wrong, and a 'police family' does actually exist, then in this case through lack of interest and apathy the 'Dysfunctional Police Family Add Insult To Injury' is perhaps more appropriate.

CHAPTER 1

I MISS THE CIRCUS BUT NOT THE CLOWNS

As a young 17-year-old I joined the West Sussex Constabulary as a cadet in 1966. I had high expectations of excitement and drama along with being a part of the much referenced 'police family'.

Any ideas of camaraderie were soon shattered because overall it was replaced by rivalry. It seemed that the majority were hell bent on promoting their own self-image to gain either promotion or a place on a specialist department. This did not apply to everyone, but anyone not set on that was, in my view, in the minority.

Over the years, I frequently saw promotions of those who were not worthy, and only occasionally did I feel that the promotion was earned and deserved. I never wanted to do anything except be an efficient and proactive constable and my record shows I achieved that. I never took the police promotion examination and therefore I was never in the running to be promoted and thus I never felt jealousy because it simply did not apply to me.

I saw many who had taken the exam and not been promoted become extremely resentful, bitter, disinterested and disillusioned caused by their being overlooked. I avoided all of those emotions because I was just not in the running or interested.

On seeing someone promoted, mostly I felt either relief that the individual would be moving on to another station away from me or pleased for them that their true worth had been recognised.

I was totally in my element and happy to be on the streets with the public. I also had an insatiable thirst to catch 'bad guys'. I still crave the adrenaline rush I got from the chase and the ultimate capture, and nothing has ever or will replace it.

I had periods on specialist departments such as CID and firearms, but I never wanted to stay and wanted to get back into uniform and on the streets again.

CID on a permanent basis never appealed to me and I found that I gained little satisfaction from the experience. This was because most of the work would come via an initial telephone call. (Yes, back then you could telephone the police and get to speak to a human!)

From that initial call I normally could tell whether the reported crime could be detected or not. Generally, it was unlikely that it could ever be detected and then one simply went through the motions and routine of recording the crime and completing the paperwork.

I also found out that the workshy would only answer the phone if forced to and busied themselves by keeping their head down as if absorbed in some report or other, seemingly oblivious to a phone ringing. They generally got away with it through those of us who could not outlast them and picked the phone up.

I soon found that those who resisted answering the phone always avoided any incoming work and were free to 'swan about' at their leisure. They also had other tricks such as they would go 'walkabout' within the police station merely engaging others in light, unrelated to the police, conversation. However, they were always careful to be seen carrying a piece of paper that was normally of no consequence. This served the purpose of giving the impression that they were on a mission related to the paper when it was nothing more than an excuse to 'skive' and a distraction.

Those who had become practiced in the magic illusion of appearing to be busy also used another trick. This consisted of having a desk full of crime files thus appearing to have many pending cases. However, if looked at more closely it could be seen that 75% were concluded cases, with only a sprinkling of current enquiries.

I despised those workshy devious types. Anyone who became my friend within police circles had to be someone I thought of as a good copper. If they were not, then I gave them a wide berth and I looked on them as a mere acquaintance or someone I was forced to tolerate.

Those types also tended to ingratiate themselves with anyone of rank and would never rock the boat. The other thing is if you do little or nothing then you will never make a mistake or be criticised. Whereas if you had a heavy workload like mine always was, then you had to be aware that on many occasions when I was congratulated, in the blink of an eye you could become the 'bogeyman' and be treated as such.

I came to be very laidback about this attitude and took both congratulations and criticism with a pinch of salt. Nothing stood in my way of catching a bad guy and never did I have any fear of repercussions. I thought that if I acted reasonably then that would ensure that I could weather any storm and overall, it worked.

Even the most minor of complaints against an officer could develop into what appeared to be a major incident and whoever was the target would be treated as being guilty and avoided. This also included those who you might be on good terms with or indeed believed to be a friend. It was a self-preservation thing and an opportunity for them to distance themselves for fear of jeopardising their own image or position. I saw this happen frequently and few examples of true camaraderie.

I have always thought that although any town has a contingent of police officers in reality that town will be policed by about 50% of its allocation. My reasoning is that only that proportion will be dedicated and hard-working coppers. The rest will be what are termed as 'uniform carriers' or in armed forces terms 'non-combatants' and a cardboard cutout would have had the same function.

I do not know what goes on nowadays but during my time in the police, 1967 to 1989, those I refer to would leave the police station and wander their beat going from 'tea spot to tea spot'. A tea spot in police terms is any place where a copper was welcomed and tea being on offer.

There was an old police disciplinary charge from a bygone era, which was referred to as 'idle gossiping'. It was a way of dealing with idle beat officers. By the time I was in the police that term although often referred to was never enforced to my knowledge, but I saw it breached daily and normally by the same ones.

These officers also had their methods of avoiding work and one that comes to mind is that in large towns at weekends and special occasions when public disturbance is expected, the police would deploy a mobile van unit with a dozen or so officers onboard. The tactic used by the shirkers would be to ensure they entered the rear of the van first. This meant that when being deployed at any rowdy incident, they would be last out of the van making sure they took their time in alighting. This gave the timid the best chance of not getting too involved and the first officer(s) alighting would likely make any necessary arrest and they could take either a spectating or if forced to an assisting role.

These officers were thus less likely to ever be injured, whereas first out of the van enthusiastic officers, such as myself, greatly enhanced their chances of being injured, as I was on many occasions. I always thought that at all stages of my connection with the Police Service that I gave more loyalty than I ever received back. I made only a handful of true count-on friends. The rest were merely people I worked with and fair-weather acquaintances as in many occupations.

I was frequently disappointed by the lack of camaraderie of many I worked alongside and by their selfishness too. I can recall times when this was glaringly apparent. Something that comes to mind is when a colleague reached his/her retirement after completing his/her 30 years of service. There would usually be a 'whip-round' to buy the retiree a farewell card and small gift, normally an engraved tankard for a male.

There were between 15 to 20 of us on a section and with me being a non-shrinking violet it usually fell to me to 'pass the hat round' in the form of an envelope. It did not appear to matter if the retiree was popular or not, the proceeds of the collection were always disappointingly meagre and often included a foreign coin or washer etc.

There was ordinarily a 'leaving do' in the social club (sadly, non-existent nowadays) and so more times than not and to avoid embarrassment, I had to apply added pressure to increase the collection or request a top-up from the social club committee.

This was indeed a sorry situation especially as the retiree had normally, at some cost, laid on a buffet and 'put money over the bar' to buy everyone at the station a farewell drink.

Often, I saw normally non-frequenters of the social club arrive as they finished at 10pm, receive a free-gratis drink and whilst remaining at the other end of the bar, give a 'thumbs-up' to the retiree, consume the drink and depart without ever approaching or uttering a word to the purchaser.

I always thought a farewell 'do' should be arranged by those remaining and not by the one departing. When it came to my turn, after being off sick for nearly a year and with few police visitors, I chose not to arrange one and as a result neither the 'do' nor I were missed.

I long ago stopped referring to all as being the 'police family' or individuals as 'my mates'. They were merely colleagues who did the same job as me.

Notwithstanding all that I have said, I still care passionately about those police officers either killed or injured on duty. No one deserves to go to work and for that to take place.

I am not bitter or sorry for myself for what happened to me injury wise. I only intend to tell of my difficult journey to seek to change UK police history and to finally achieve proper recognition for severely injured police officers. As my campaign still continues as I write this, I will record happenings as they occur.

There will never be a better time than right now to run this campaign, even though we are all aware of the current decline in the reputation of the once world respected 'British Bobby'. Much of the over-the-top damaging media reports are exaggerated and sensationalised because it's that which sells newspapers and not the good work of police officers.

I believe that the frontline constables are not to blame in any way for the often-poor service on offer. The fault lies with underfunding, under staffing and the lack of proper leadership from the top. We live in ever increasing turbulent times which puts added pressure on police resources, but we must value the commitment of many police officers who endeavour to keep us safe and often that means they put themselves in harm's way to protect us. With this in mind, I believe that any police officer who sacrifices their life or health should receive proper recognition and that for far too long has not been the case.

We frequently hear outlandish references to the untrustworthiness of police officers and inferences that all are potential sex offenders or murderers. I am outraged by the statements I read. The police will never win any popularity awards only because of the type of job it is. On percentages alone it shows that most officers are decent people in exactly the same way as the rest of the population.

When Dr Harold Shipman killed what is thought to be 400 + good folks and it hit the news was it said, 'All doctors were killers' and did everyone stop keeping appointments with them? When the serial killer Peter Sutcliffe was caught, was an accusing finger pointed at every lorry driver? Of course not, but when it comes to the police it presents an opportunity to those who are uninformed and/or anti-police to make derogatory comments and unfounded accusations purely because they want to and can.

I can tell you that during my time as a copper, I never encountered a bent or racist officer. I was only ever interested in collaring bad guys irrespective of nationality, colour or beliefs and to the best of my knowledge that was the same for all my colleagues.

Like all of us, I hear horror stories of there being cases that contradict what I say but all I am saying is that I never came across any of it.

CHAPTER 2

THE 200-YEAR-OLD SCANDAL

Hopefully, I have now given a bit of background in order for me to shortly proceed with the main topic of this book which is to describe how many officers are often severely injured and even more sadly killed too, whilst carrying out their day-to-day duties in seeking to protect the public. The great majority of these officers never receive any form of medal recognition for their health or life sacrifice.

This book will predominantly focus on my campaign for the injured, albeit I also strongly support the award of posthumous medals.

Later, I will detail several harrowingly sad cases of brave officers who unfortunately suffered life-changing injuries and the lack of recognition of their health sacrifice.

Many high-profile cases of injured officers normally involve those related to either shooting or stabbing because they command more attention due only to the dramatic way the harm is sustained and thus will garner much more public interest

However, let us not forget that the great majority of injuries sustained by officers are often caused in the most simplistic of ways, such as everyday straightforward physical assault, as in for example punching, kicking or in road traffic accidents. Whilst these cases will undoubtedly receive considerably less publicity than the former, they certainly deserve the same degree of recognition and indeed sympathy. I submit that it is not the manner in which the injuries are caused but the degree that should be focused on.

I want to make it perfectly clear at the outset that when I refer to the 'injured on duty', also included are those who are unfortunate enough to suffer from post-traumatic stress disorder. (PTSD).

The definition in police terms when referring to an 'injury on duty award' is 'any injury of body or mind, or partially contributing towards and causing permanent incapacity'. Therefore, from this moment on when 'injury on duty' is referenced then be aware that it does most definitely include PTSD.

PTSD is still to be recognised by many in the same way as a physical injury. Only in modern times has it been accepted as being a genuine and serious complaint but in my view it still has some way to go.

It must be remembered that only a little over 100 years ago, during WW1, young men suffering from PTSD, often referred to as shellshock, were wrongly labelled as cowards and 'shot at dawn'.

I do not suffer from PTSD, but I experienced it firsthand when my nephew, who is not a police officer, developed horrendous symptoms after being injured at work. He changed from a reliable hard-working and devoted husband and father, into someone no one recognised. He developed a drink problem, and his teenage sweetheart bride and long-term wife, sought refuge in a battered wives' home. Happily, in his case, there is light at the end of the tunnel and he and the family are learning to cope with it.

I believe unless you unfortunately suffer from the illness yourself or have frequent contact with someone and step by step witness the development, then you may never truly understand the complexity of the extremely debilitating problem. We should not forget either the family members of the sufferer, who also have their lives turned upside down and are tortured too. So having outlined my concerns for the injured before we move on, I must highlight the fact that my views are identical for the unfortunate officers who are also killed. However, a campaign to seek recognition for the 'fallen' is already separately underway.

What caused alarm and instigated the start of my campaign was when I discovered the Police Federation for England and Wales (PFEW or known in police circles as the, Fed.) were fully supporting a posthumous campaign for the 'fallen' but once again the severely injured were overlooked and forgotten as if being irrelevant. I'm sure that is not the case and is only an oversight and not a deliberate act. However, it is certain to cause added distress to all those who were injured.

Upon reading the report on the posthumous award campaign, which was reported via the PFEW website, I decided that I should once again resurrect the campaign for the injured which I attempted 20+ years ago but had to abandon due to not being able to broadcast it widely, it being the era of pre-social media. That of course is not so now.

Here follows the PFEW report in full. It should be read to understand the criterion of the posthumous campaign and it should then be clear to see why my proposal is of equal importance.

MPs CALL ON NUMBER 10 TO CREATE 'ELIZABETH MEDAL' FOR FALLEN EMERGENCY WORKERS.

10 January 2023.

'An 'Elizabeth Medal' awarded to the families of emergency workers who have lost their lives in the line of duty is one step closer to becoming reality, as the campaign continues to gather momentum with the backing of a number of Parliamentarians.

Today in Parliament [10 January 2023], a multitude of cross-party MPs held a backbench debate, secured by Wendy Chamberlain, Liberal Democrat MP and chief whip and spokesperson for work and pensions, to push the Police Federation of England and Wales's (PFEW) Medals for Heroes campaign.

PFEW is pressing for Home Office approval and is seeking cross-party support to enhance the current honours and awards system, which fails to adequately reflect the dedication, commitment and sacrifice of those individuals who lost their lives in keeping their communities safe.

It would be similar in status to the Elizabeth Cross, which is awarded to the bereaved relatives of members of the British Armed Forces killed in military action.

Moving a motion, Ms. Chamberlain told MPs: "We have long-standing awards for gallantry, sacrifice and service, for those who have given to our country in all sorts of different ways. It is right that such service deserves recognition, and the recipients and their families are rightly proud.

But sadly, there are those who have equally served their country and have made sacrifices who are not being recognised as they should.

No reward or recognition can replace the loss of a loved one, but if we can go some way to make them feel like that loss has been recognised, it is very important."

She spoke of how she joined Lothian and Borders Police in 1999, serving for 12 years as a police officer, as were her father and husband. All of them suffered violent assault.

Her father also won a Royal Humane Society award in 1983 for rescuing a man from drowning in a dock.

The Medals for Heroes campaign was officially launched by PFEW, the Police Superintendents' Association and the Prison Officers' Association in April last year.

The campaign has also been supported by Bryn Hughes, whose daughter PC Nicola Hughes and her colleague PC Fiona Bone were murdered 10 years ago, and the families of fallen officers across the United Kingdom, including the family of PC George Taylor.

PC George Taylor who served Police Scotland was killed on 30 November 1976 by Robert Mone and Thomas McCulloch.

In 2021, they were told by the Secretary of State for Scotland, Alistair Jack, their latest request for a medal had been disappointingly refused by the Home Office and Cabinet Office in Downing Street.

"There are many families with ongoing campaigns for justice. That is why I am here with other members, calling on the Government to institute a new award for emergency service workers," Ms. Chamberlain continued.

"It is part of the royal prerogative to determine honours and awards, but the Prime Minister does give advice on such matters, so I would argue that it is entirely within the Government and Prime Minister's purview to put forward the recommendations, endorsed not only by members in this place, but professional bodies across the country for a new award."

Fallen Nottinghamshire Police Constable Ged Walker was also remembered during the debate.

On 7 January 2003, PC Walker was dragged 100 yards and fatally injured by a stolen taxi as he reached into the vehicle in an attempt to remove the keys from the ignition. He died in hospital two days later from serious head injuries. He was survived by his widow and two children.

Darren Henry, Conservative MP for Broxtowe, said: "PC Walker is a shining example of why an award, such as a medal, should exist. He and all other police officers put their lives on the line every day they go to work. Officers who have lost their lives protecting their communities must be recognised in such tragic circumstances."

Holly Lynch, Labour MP for Halifax and shadow minister for security, commented: "So often officers are out there on their own. There is no such thing as a routine call in policing - the circumstances can change in an instant.

This medal will be one step towards understanding the contributions they make, the risks that they take, and what we really owe to the families of those who have made the ultimate sacrifice in the line of duty."

I submit that all that was said also applies to the seriously injured.

Whilst the PFEW fully support the posthumous campaign, you will read further on of my arduous task to reach them and to encourage the same for my campaign for the injured.

So, having read that comprehensive report which undoubtedly will provide better understanding of the concerns, we can now move on.

Since the Metropolitan Police Service as we know it was formed in 1829, there has been over 5,000+ officers who have died on duty. I have no up to date figures to hand of the severely injured but I do know that in 2015 there were 15,853 officers in the UK who had been discharged from the service on medical grounds as the result of sustaining severe injuries whilst carrying out their duties.

Based on 15,853 in 2015, I think it is safe to assume that in the past 200 years there have been hundreds of thousands of officers severely injured.

What is astounding is that only a handful of those officers, be it posthumously or otherwise, were ever recognised with a medal award. Initially, I too was shocked by that but after I explain why the reason will become apparent.

The only medals available are, The George Cross, The George Medal, The King's Gallantry Medal and the King's Police Medal. The criterion for ALL these awards is that there must be a high degree of gallantry displayed to be a recipient. There lies the problem because the vast majority of officers are deprived of opportunity to display any form of gallantry because they are attacked instantly and without warning. Therefore, if there is no gallantry there is no medal. It's as simple as that.

Let me give you a few examples of those who because of the strict criterion of the awards received no medal whatsoever in recognition of their sacrifice.

In 1984, Yvonne Fletcher was fatally wounded by a shot fired from the Libyan embassy in St James's Square, London, by an unknown gunman. No one has ever been arrested or charged with the offence of murder.

In 2005 in Bradford, PCs Sharon Beshenivsky and Teresa Milburn were shot when attending a bank alarm. Sadly, Sharon died but Teresa was saved.

In 2010, Northumbrian PC David Rathband was shot in the face at point-blank range with a shotgun. He was of course seriously wounded and blinded. Sadly, he took his own life subsequently.

In 2012, in Greater Manchester, PCs Fiona Bone and Nicola Hughes were both fatally shot, and a hand-grenade thrown at them. Nicola's father, Bryn Hughes, started the posthumous award campaign and recently I have often spoken with him.

In all of the above cases it was not possible to show any form of gallantry because the officers were attacked without warning. They were not eligible for, nor did they receive any medal recognition whatsoever, simply because there is no such award available.

I am confident that you will agree that to have police officers killed or maimed on the streets of the UK in the 21st century and for them to not receive any form of medal recognition is a national disgrace. It has gone on for 200 years and needs to be corrected right now.

The families of those killed have nothing to display on the right-hand side of their chest to indicate the loss of their loved one. A parent or a child would, I am sure, want a posthumous medal.

A severely injured officer who is medically discharged from the service will also have no medal to display on the left side of the chest. That officer may not have reached the eligibility period to receive their 'Long Service and Good Conduct (LS & GC) Medal' and ONLY due to the injury is deprived of that award.

Prior to 2010, the eligibility period was 22 years but thereon after it was reduced to 20 years in line with the armed forces.

If either of the next of kin of a 'fallen' officer or the severely injured officer themself attends an event such as the Police Memorial Day or a similar event, anyone viewing them could be forgiven for thinking they were nothing more than a mere spectating member of the public rather than someone who sacrificed so much. Any unknown police officer would be of the same opinion if they saw them too.

The injured without any medal will see their colleagues proudly wearing their LS & GC Medal whilst they have nothing to display showing any connection to the Police Service.

Back in 1989, I too was an injured on duty officer. Of course, then the LS & GC Medal period was 22 years but guess how close I got? Within a few weeks! I failed to receive the award because I was deprived of reaching the 22 years threshold ONLY due to the injury. In fact, I had been connected to the Police Service for 23 and a half years because I had been a police cadet for 18 months, but the cadet service did not count towards the eligibility period.

I will continue to boycott ALL police remembrance events not because I do not wish to pay my respects to the 'fallen' but because I will not be part of any such event until proper recognition is shown to those unfortunates who paid the ultimate sacrifice and lost their lives.

I have seen Prime Ministers, Home Secretaries and Chief Police Officers, bowing their heads in prayer at the services. In my opinion they should be bowing their heads in shame, knowing what is going on in the wings and appearing to be totally impervious to the disgrace. I do not do insincerity or farces!

However, there is something else that shows the unfairness and inequality of the LS & GC Medal system. Another officer may be seen proudly wearing the medal and we might find that they were a special constable. Their medal award is received after only 9 years' service with the criterion being that they have carried out a minimum of 200 hours of performed police service per year i.e. 9 X 200 equates to 1800 hours.

My completed hours over 21 years totals 43,680 hours (not including overtime) AND I sustained a life-changing injury, but I and others still received no medal.

Is it any wonder that an injured on duty officer who is medically discharged from the service feels overlooked and devalued, given the unfairness and the health sacrifice they have made.

I only give my personal example because it appropriately highlights the issue. There are far too many others similarly affected and with much more severe injuries than myself and I will now detail many of the harrowingly sad experiences.

The following stories are of those who sacrificed their health and jobs to keep us all safe. I have done little or no editing because I want what is related to reach the reader in its original form. Please bear in mind as you read on that some are suffering from a brain injury or may be suffering from post-traumatic stress disorder.

I thought I had heard and seen much of that suffered but I must admit even I was stunned and saddened by what I discovered.

It is important to read the stories to understand my passion and the need to mount a campaign to seek proper recognition for those who have been overlooked for 200 years.

CHAPTER 3

THE FORGOTTEN INJURED

It is crucially important to first read and gain knowledge of the harrowingly sad stories of those police officers who have sacrificed their health in their efforts to keep us all safe, prior to reading the progress and the difficulties of my campaign only then will the reader fully understand the necessity of it.

The first story is of a Metropolitan police officer.

PC Philip Olds

On 23 December 1980, traffic officer PC Philip Olds of the Metropolitan Police stumbled across biker Stuart Blackstock and an accomplice robbing an off-licence in Hayes, West London. When challenged, Blackstock produced a handgun, pointed it at the officer and shot him at point-blank range. Philip suffered severe spinal damage and was left paralysed, and wheelchair bound.

A manhunt soon had Blackstock in custody, and then put on trial. To the astonishment of everybody, Blackstock was cleared of attempted murder but convicted of wounding PC Olds with intent. The report in the Daily Mirror said that Blackstock smiled when cleared of attempted murder. He received a minimum sentence of seventeen years.

PC Olds was awarded the Queen's Gallantry Medal.

Twenty years later, Blackstock received compensation because his parole hearing was delayed at length, and to the disgust of the Police, received around £6,000.

Blackstock was paroled in 2002, claiming that he had apologised to the Olds family and wanted to rebuild his life.

PC Olds did not fare so well. In 1986, he was found dead from a drink and drugs overdose. It was said that he could not come to terms with his being paralysed, a case eerily echoed recently by the suicide of PC David Rathband, an officer blinded when shot in the face by the monster Raoul Moat.

The Bombing Outside Harrods.

On the afternoon of 17 December 1983, IRA members parked a car containing a bomb near the side entrance of Harrods, on Hans Crescent, London. The bomb exploded at about 13:21, as four police officers in a car, an officer on foot and a police dog-handler neared the suspect vehicle.

Six people were killed (three officers and three bystanders) and 90 others were injured, including 9 children and 14 police officers. The blast damaged 24 cars and all five floors on the side of Harrods. The police car absorbed much of the blast and this likely prevented further casualties.

The huge impact ripped through Hans Crescent, which was crowded with Christmas shoppers. A warning had been received but the bomb device exploded as the police were attempting to clear the area. The next day the IRA admitted to placing the car bomb and a few days later they expressed their 'regret' saying that the operation had not been authorised.

Harrods shop windows were blown out causing severe injuries to staff and customers. Despite the damage, the store re-opened three days later, vowing not to be defeated by acts of terrorism.

In 1984 the Police Memorial Trust was set up to erect memorials to those officers killed on duty at or near the place where they fell. The film director and Kensington resident, Michael Winner, was the founder of the charitable trust which is run from an office in Kensington High Street.

One of the first memorials to be erected was to those killed by the IRA bomb in 1983. Princess Alexandra performed the unveiling on 24 September 1985. Lord Whitelaw represented the Government and gave a short speech.

The families of Inspector Stephen Dodd, Police Sergeant Noel Lane and Woman Police Constable Jane Arbuthnot all attended the ceremony. Margaret Thatcher, then Prime Minister, and Neil Kinnock, then Leader of the Opposition, attended later to pay their respects and lay flowers. The Royal Borough of Kensington and Chelsea later commissioned a similar tablet in remembrance of the three innocent civilians who died - Philip Gededes, Kenneth Gerald Salvesen and Jasmine Cochran Patrick - which was placed immediately above the Memorial to the Police Officers.

There were no medals awarded to any of the killed or injured for what they suffered that sad day.

PCs Sharon Beshenivsky and Teresa Milburn

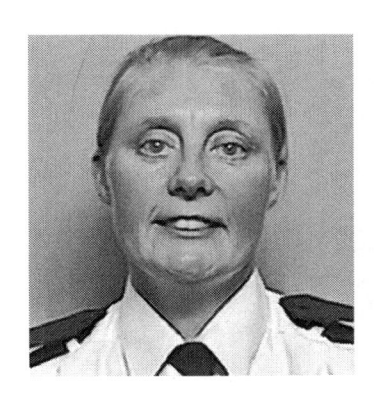

PC Sharon Beshenivsky

PC Teresa Milburn

I include this next story because although Sharon was killed Teresa survived her injuries and therefore it fits the criterion linked to the campaign and book.

I frequently reference this case due to it being a big part of my argument for my medal proposal. If or when the pending posthumous award proposal is approved and if it is made retrospectively, then Sharon will receive her long over-due medal recognition.

However, Teresa will once again be forgotten unless my proposal for the injured is also approved. The ignoring of Teresa would be totally unfair and unacceptable, and everything must be done to prevent the repeated snub.

Given that Sharon and Teresa attended the same incident, they acted jointly, and their actions were identical, I ask this question; 'how can anyone support a posthumous medal for Sharon without considering the award of a medal to Teresa?'

On the afternoon of 18 November 2005, PCs Sharon Beshenivsky and Teresa Milburn responded to a report that an attack alarm had been activated at a travel agency on Morley Street in Bradford, West Yorkshire.

Upon arrival at the scene, the officers encountered three men who had robbed the agent of £5,405; two were armed with a gun, another with a knife. One of the gunmen fired at them immediately at point-blank range fatally wounding Beshenivsky in the chest and also hitting Milburn in the chest, before all three men made a getaway in a convoy of cars.

Teresa was seriously injured. She had joined the force less than two years earlier. Sharon had served only nine months as a Constable, having been a Community Support Officer before.

PC Sharon Beshenivsky (née Jagger; 14 January 1967 – 18 November 2005) was the seventh female officer to die in the line of duty in England and Wales and the second female officer to be fatally shot (the first was Yvonne Fletcher in London in 1984).

She had three children and two stepchildren and died on her youngest daughter's fourth birthday. Sharon's funeral took place on 6 January 2006 at Bradford Cathedral.

Closed-circuit television cameras tracked a car rushing from the scene and used an automatic number plate recognition system to trace its owners. This led to six suspects being arrested; three were later convicted of murder, robbery, and firearms offences; two of manslaughter, robbery, and firearms offences; and one of robbery.

On 25 November 2005 police named Somali brothers Mustaf Jama, aged 25, and Yusaf Jama, aged 19, as well as 24-year-old Pakistani Muzzaker Imtiaz Shah as prime suspects. Yusaf Jama was arrested in Birmingham the following day and was subsequently charged with murder and robbery.

On 12 December Shah was arrested in Newport, South Wales. He was later also charged with murder. Mustaf Jama had fled to Somalia but was extradited two years later.

The use of recently installed automatic number plate recognition technology in Bradford city centre played a vital role in identifying the suspects prior to their arrest.

More than 14 years after the crime, in January 2020, another suspect was arrested in Islamabad, Pakistan. Piran Dhitta Khan, age 71 at the time of his arrest, was reported to be wanted for masterminding the robbery. British police were granted his extradition in April 2023.

Convictions/Sentences

On 18 December 2006, Yusuf Jama was found guilty of all charges against him, including the murder of Beshenivsky. He was sentenced to life imprisonment with a minimum term of 35 years. This was expected to keep Yusuf Jama imprisoned until at least 2040 and the age of 60.

Mustaf Jama: murder; robbery; firearms. He was given a life sentence with a 35-year tariff. On 1 November 2007 Mustaf Jama had been extradited from Somalia, after a Home Office funded snatch operation that involved his Land Rover being ambushed by 15 local militiamen and then Jama being flown by private plane to the UK via Dubai and taken into police custody at Bridewell police station in Leeds. He was charged the next day with the murder of Beshenivsky, and appeared before Leeds magistrates, and was remanded into custody.

On 22 July 2009 at Newcastle Crown Court, he was found guilty of murder and was also told that he would serve at least 35 years in prison, which is expected to keep him in prison until 2044 and the age of 64. It later transpired that he had been released from prison (having been convicted of burglary and robbery offences) just six months before Beshenivsky's murder and that he had been considered for deportation to his native Somalia.

Yusuf Jama: murder; robbery; firearms. He was sentenced to life imprisonment with a 35-year tariff.

Muzzaker Shah: murder; robbery; firearms. Shah was also sentenced to life imprisonment with a minimum term of 35 years, which was also expected to keep him in prison until at least 2040 and the age of 60.

Faisal Razzaq: manslaughter; robbery; firearms. Faisal Razzaq, a 25-year-old from London, was cleared of murder but found guilty of manslaughter. He was sentenced to life imprisonment with a minimum term of 11 years before being considered for parole. This was expected to keep him imprisoned until at least 2017 and the age of 36. He had driven the lead car of the gang's convoy from Leeds to Bradford and acted as a lookout during the robbery.

Hassan Razzaq: manslaughter; robbery; firearms. On 2 March 2007, Hassan Razzaq, the 26-year-old brother of Faisal, was also convicted of manslaughter and was sentenced to 20 years in prison. He had also acted as a lookout. Raza Ul-Haq Aslam was a 3rd lookout and was sentenced to eight years in prison for a single robbery offence.

All of the suspects except Aslam were also found guilty of robbery and a series of firearms offences.

Yusuf Jama and Muzzaker Shah appealed for their sentences to be reduced. The High Court heard their appeals but agreed with the trial judge's recommended minimum term for both men and rejected the appeals. In 2010 Mustaf Jama also had his appeal rejected.

Hewan Gordon was jailed for 18 months in 2007 for helping Shah evade capture. In 2010 he won an appeal against a Government bid to deport him back to Somalia. His appeal was understood to have been made on human rights' grounds.

In relation to Khan, in 2014, police renewed their appeal for information that might lead to Khan's arrest. Detective Superintendent Simon Atkinson said: "This investigation is not yet complete and will not be until everyone involved in any way in the murder of PC Beshenivsky is brought to justice. We have not and will not leave any stone unturned in our search for justice. The £20,000 reward on offer remains and I would like to take this opportunity to appeal again to the people of Pakistan or to anyone who knows where this man is to get in contact."

Khan was arrested in Pakistan on 14 January 2020. He appeared in court in Islamabad the following day and was remanded in custody until 29 January.

In April 2023 Khan was extradited to the UK and taken to a West Yorkshire police station, where he was charged with murder, robbery, two counts of possessing a firearm with intent to endanger life and two counts of possessing a prohibited weapon. He was remanded in custody to appear at Westminster Magistrates' Court on 13 April 2023.

In June 2007, Shah had nine years added to his sentence for firearms' offences committed during a car chase in 2004. Faisal Razzaq had seven-and-a-half-years added to his sentence in June 2007 for possession of firearms in 2004.

In December 2007, Yusuf Jama was also convicted of conspiracy to rape and had 12 years added to his sentence. The case related to the gang rape of a woman at a house party in Birmingham some days after Beshenivsky's murder.

In March 2008, both Shah and Yusuf Jama had a further four years added to their sentences for wounding with intent after they stabbed another inmate at Frankland prison in Brasside, County Durham.

On 8 May 2009, a memorial to Beshenivsky was unveiled at the location of her death. At the unveiling, Prime Minister Gordon Brown paid tribute to the officer's "dedication, professionalism and courage". Michael Winner, chairman of the Police Memorial Trust, also praised Beshenivsky and police officers across the country, saying: "Take them away and there's total anarchy and we are devoured by the forces of evil."

I primarily included this case because Teresa survived and continued with her police service and became a detective. I have failed to find out any more of what became of her. I emailed West Yorkshire Police, but I received no reply. I hope she is safe, well and thriving.

Neither of the 2 officers received any medal recognition.

The next story sparked one of the biggest manhunts in police history. Many of you will recall the sickening tale of horrendously injured PC David Rathband. Sadly, David is no longer with us.

PCs David Rathband

PC David Rathband

On July 3, 2010, only 2 days after being released from Durham prison, 37-year-old Northumbrian, Raul Moat shot and wounded his ex-girlfriend Samantha Stobbart, 22, with a sawn-off shotgun and killed her new boyfriend Chris Brown, 29.

Samantha had wrongly told Moat that Chris was a serving police officer because she quite rightly feared reprisals for ditching him. Rather than having the desired effect of deterring Moat from seeking revenge it further enraged his hatred for the police. Tree surgeon and club bouncer Moat had in the past sought psychiatric help.

The following day, Moat phoned 999 to "declare war" on the police.

About 10 minutes later, close to East Denton, he shot Northumbrian Police traffic officer PC David Rathband in the face blinding him. At the time David was parked up and sitting in his police car.

Moat then went on the run sparking a nationwide manhunt seeking to capture him. He headed to Rothbury, Northumberland and was eventually tracked down camping-out in a rural area that he knew well. 7 days after the shootings and surrounded by armed police, 2 stun-guns were fired in the hope of subduing him, but he turned the shotgun on himself and was killed.

David suffered catastrophic injuries including the loss of his sight. In the following months he battled with his appalling injuries, and he inspired the nation with his determination to return to the job he loved.

His 20-year marriage to his wife, Kath, failed and the couple separated. They had a son and a daughter together.

In February 2012, 2 days after returning from visiting his twin brother in Australia, sadly David succumbed to his understandable depression, and he took his own life at his home in Blyth.

He had set-up a charity to help other stricken emergency services personnel and went on to win a Daily Mirror Pride of Britain award for his bravery at a celebrity-packed ceremony.

He wrote his own autobiography and spent huge amounts of time fundraising and making public appearances after setting up the Blue Lamp Foundation, which still exists today.

Note that on the photograph, David does not display any medal. That is because he never received one in recognition of his sacrifice.

Undoubtedly, if had he lived and been medically discharged from the police, he would have qualified for my medal proposal.

The next story is of West Yorkshire lass, Angie McLoughlin who was attacked in 1982. She left the service with no medal to show any connection to the Police Service or for her health sacrifice. The poor soul has suffered the consequences for 40 years.

She sustained severe brain damage and is confined to a wheelchair.

I have known her for several years, through an injured police group but we have never met. We speak regularly on the telephone. I greatly admire her upbeat character and pleasant disposition. She shows love and care to everyone she meets, and I consider her to be a loyal and trusted friend.

She is the one who inspired and continues to motivate me every day to continue with the campaign to seek due recognition for her extreme sacrifice which has lasted for 40 years.

Angie McLoughlin

Angie McLoughlin

This is my story of being a policewoman, being attacked, sustaining life-changing injuries and not being able due to my injury on duty to continue my employment and get a medal for long service.

I joined the West Yorkshire Police in 1977. I had wanted to join since I was 13 years old. Then I got married before I was 18, so that was that! The Equal Rights Act came in during 1975, which allowed married women to join the Police. I waited another 2 years until my son was 10 years old before I could fulfil my 'life's dream!' I was 27 and not a young 'un.

I was just going back to the station with my colleague one night, whilst working for a month undercover, 12 noon to midnight, checking car parks.

It was 11.45pm and this was our last night carrying out this duty. We had done well and had locked up a lot of car thieves, and those breaking into cars for whatever they could find. We were walking towards a crossroads where we would take a left turn. We saw at the last minute 3 men walking towards us. They had huge bundles under both their arms. We knew they had broken into a clothes store. I whispered to my colleague that I would take the one on the right and he could pick which one he wanted to grab. The guy in the centre was middle-aged, and HUGE!

I took the guy on the right, and the other two ran off. They dropped their bundles, so the stuff was all over the road. The bundles were all fur and leather coats. I turned my head to check my colleague. He only had about 18 months service in, and he had run after the other 2 guys.

I felt the first punch at the back of my neck. I think what they call a 'rabbit punch'. It stunned me but I managed to hold onto him. I was NOT going to lose a prisoner! He was battering me around the back of my head, which I kept down, now hanging onto him with both hands, grabbing his clothing to prevent his escape. These were my thoughts as this hammering was going on:

'Wow I can't even feel this, how come it doesn't hurt at all?' and 'You can do this all night, you are NOT getting away from me'.

Then I realised that we were on different radio signals. I was on the one to the station. I knew I had to get my radio out and call backup. It took me about 5 seconds to call in, "10-13, the Head row", twice.

Then it seemed I was watching from above what he was doing to me, and then off I went up a beautiful tunnel! That is all I am saying about that. But it seems in that few seconds he had broken my nose, split my lip right through, with the corner of my nostril going with it and given me two black eyes.

I was 'back again' for a few seconds and knew I was going to die if I did not stop him! I went for his face with my fingernails. Then I was gone again.

It seems he had just leaned forward and slipped out of all his upper clothing, a sheepskin coat, a sweatshirt and a T-shirt. He had run off naked from the waist up in January. I still had it all in my hands and apparently it had taken my inspector 10 minutes to get it free from me.

I was taken to hospital. They stitched my lip and that was it, no x-rays. Nothing after that. It took 26 years before the severe brain damage was diagnosed.

All I knew was that I was not the same person who had been attacked. There was no longer anything 'normal' about me! I have no quality of life and if it was not for my devoted husband, Graham, life would not be worth living.

After being on the 'injury on duty' (IOD) pension, Band 1, for 22 years, it took 15 years more of battling the 'police pensions' authority', (PPA) via the courts to gain justice and the correct banding of the injury on duty award.

I was retired on Band 1 IOD pension at 25%. They decided after 20 years to review me! I was placed on Band 4 at 88%. That was some review, eh?

Author's comment.

Poor Angie's life changed for the worse that night forty years ago and she continues to suffer from the effects of her cowardly attack.

Shockingly, she spent nearly a lifetime battling the PPA to obtain her correct IOD award.

It is also totally outrageous that her bravery and health sacrifice remain unrecognised and that she left the service without a medal.

Martin Gill

Martin Gill

I joined the West Midlands Police in 1985 and I became Police Constable 8966 Martin Gill and began a job I came to love.

I was engaged on uniform mobile patrol on my own on 18th February 1988.

At this time, I responded to what came through as a routine alarm call. This in fact turned out to be an armed robbery at Caldmore post office, Walsall. Initially and upon arriving at the scene, the postmaster advised me that someone was locked inside the post office. Unfortunately for me and upon entering the building the same postmaster locked me inside with the suspect. It was after a brief search that I found the suspect hiding behind the post office counter. He was holding a sawn-off shotgun and was also armed with a machete. A violent struggle then ensued with the offender.

During this struggle I had to hit the offender repeatedly across the body and eventually the head with a truncheon. At one stage the offender pointed the gun at me and pulled the trigger but luckily for me it did not go off. I was literally in a fight for my life which lasted several minutes.

Sadly, the CID officer who dealt with the case, never considered my actions, but regrettably listened to a convicted serial criminal and accused me of using excessive force against the suspect and being overzealous.

I was subjected to a formal complaint's procedure, which caused severe stress and anxiety. The complaint was found to be unsubstantiated, and I returned to duty.

The offender received a long custodial sentence. Some years later he escaped custody and was found deceased in Holland.

I received no recognition at the time for my arrest and it was not until 21 years later, on 17 September 2009, that the Chief Constable at that time awarded me a retrospective Chief Constable's Commendation.

It reads as follows:

Chief Constable's Commendation

Awarded to Constable 8966 Martin Gill

For your actions on 18th February 1988 when you attended the scene of an armed robbery at a post office in Walsall. The offender was armed with a sawn-off shotgun and several bladed weapons including a machete. Despite a violent struggle you bravely and without thought for your own safety arrested him. This is an excellent example of protecting the public and helping those in need.

D Thompson

Chief Constable

Date: 17th September 2009

Prior to joining West Midlands Police, I had served for 8 years in the Armed Forces and saw three years' active service in Northern Ireland during the height of the Troubles. Nothing I encountered there compared to the fear and horror I experienced on the day of that robbery.

Some months passed and on 11th September the same year I was involved in an incident described at the time by the Divisional Commander on the main TV news networks as a 'Mini Hungerford'.

A young man armed with a sawn-off shotgun went on the rampage in Walsall town centre shooting several members of the public before taking his own life just feet in front of me.

In the January of the following year, I was seriously injured after attending a burglary (alone).

By far the most serious incident was on 26th January 1989. I was alone on mobile patrol when I responded to a burglary in progress.

As I arrived on scene, two suspects fled in a stolen vehicle. This culminated in a short pursuit, which ended abruptly when the driver lost control of the vehicle hitting a wall outside a public house on a notorious estate.

I tried to radio for assistance whilst struggling with the driver of the vehicle, but unbeknownst to me my radio messages did not get through. I was in a radio black spot.

Whilst engaging in a violent struggle with the driver, the passenger had entered the public house and emerged with a group of men, too many in number for me to recall exactly. I was set upon being punched and kicked to the ground. My legs were pinned down and pulled apart and I was repeatedly kicked between the legs resulting in the loss of a testicle.

I was stabbed in my right thigh and then dragged to the side of the road where my left knee was fractured by placing my leg against the kerb. I lost consciousness on several occasions and believed I was going to be killed.

Fortunately, an elderly woman who lived in a bungalow overlooking the scene reported the ongoing assault to the station by phone. She probably saved my life.

Only two offenders were convicted of wounding, and both received lengthy custodial sentences.

It was this incident that caused me to receive multiple injuries, including the loss of a testicle, multiple lacerations and a puncture wound from a screwdriver. I also sustained a severe knee injury.

I appreciate that as police officers we all understand the dangers we may face and it's part of the job.

There are many other incidents I was involved in and in fact my personal records will show a host of chief superintendent's commendations and a chief constable's commendation for bravery during an incident involving football violence when a young man was murdered in front of me.

Sadly, for me, the Walsall post office incident, which had the most impact, damaged me mentally but that got the least attention and no recognition.

There's a lot more to my own personal story, but in short, I was seriously injured. My injuries included being stabbed, sustaining a serious injury to my left knee, back and groin. The groin injury resulted in the loss of a testicle. I also sustained various other superficial wounds. I've had over twenty surgeries over the years, the most recent in 2020. I was later diagnosed with PTSD and Chronic Anxiety.

I received no support and in fact I had to fight the Police Pensions'

Authority to receive the correct 'injury on duty' pension award. I felt worthless and undervalued. I believe I deserved better treatment for my service than I received.

I had 8 years' Royal Military Police service and 11 years' Police pensionable service, 20 years in total. The eligibility period for the police ' Long Service and Good Conduct Medal' at that time was 22 years.

As I was short of that I left with no medal recognition whatsoever to show any connection to the Police Service, let alone my health sacrifice.

I was pensioned off with an injury pension in 1997. All bar two of the below incidents occurred whilst I was single manned in a patrol vehicle.

My certificate of disablement states:

The condition(s) referred to in the annexed report (Certificate) is the result of an injury received in the execution of duty. If some conditions are and some conditions are not the result of an injury, please specify:

1. Loss of Left testicle (IOD dated 26.1.89)

2. Injury to left knee (IOD dated 26.1.89)

3. Traction injury to right arm (IOD between 23.7.96 and 25.7.96)

4. Injury to back and neck (IOD dated 23.7.96 and 25.7.96)

5. Chronic Anxiety/Post Traumatic Stress Disorder

My injuries in more detail:

- 23rd May 1987: Bitten by offender causing laceration to right finger and abrasions to right knee.
- 17th November 1987: Cuts to hands, legs and head during arrest of offender.

- 18th February 1988. Violent struggle with offender at the scene of an armed robbery at the post office where offender was armed with sawn-off shotgun & multiple bladed weapons.

- 28th February 1988: Lacerations to right calf, bruising to thighs and cuts on right hand.

- 16th July 1988: Assaulted whilst attempting to arrest offender resulting in bruised eye, fractured jaw and swollen face.

- 11th September 1988: Witness to an incident where teenager shot himself in the head with a sawn-off shotgun.

- 31st December 1988: Kick mark on right shin.

- 26th January 1989: Abrasion to forehead/face, gash to right shin requiring sutures, scratched legs and swollen testicles, puncture/stab wound right thigh, fracture to left knee.

- 13th June 1989: Sprain to right foot while chasing suspect.

- 11th October 1990: Kicked at scene of public disorder causing swollen right knee.

- 28th November 1993: Broken finger during arrest.

- 9th April 1995: Bottle thrown by offender causing 2nd cut to elbow requiring sutures.

- 16th March 1996: Blow to right eye and cuts to hand.

- 23rd July 1996: Lower back injury caused by fall while searching building.

- 25th July 1996: Walking with dog over rough ground. Broken wrist/severe traction injury right wrist/arm.

Author's comment.

I and many others have been stunned by poor Martin's misfortune and his long, sad catalogue of injuries. (They are included in full as an indication of how frequent they can be sustained.)

He was indeed a very proactive, dedicated and extremely brave officer.

He was seriously let down by his senior officers in that he received no gallantry award for the post office incident when he fought for his life against a male much bigger than himself. He surely escaped being killed by striking the offender with his truncheon. It's unbelievable that for his exemplary courage in making the arrest, he was suspended for the use of his truncheon.

Clearly no senior officer had the common sense to ignore the ludicrous complaint and lift his suspension, which lasted months! Why did it take that long I ask? There was only Martin and the offender in the post office at the time of the arrest. There was no one else to see and even if there was, it could have been resolved in minutes.

Instead, the poor officer was suspended from duty and left to worry about his fate for a long 6 months. Is the system trying to deter the apprehension of law breakers or encourage it?

Now there is another aspect to this fiasco and very relevant to this campaign. The reason so many officers are not considered for a medal award is because there must be a high degree of gallantry displayed.

Well it's as plain as the nose on your face that there was gallantry displayed by the bucket load in this instance. How much more has there to be than an officer fighting for his life against a man with a sawn-off shotgun, who pulls the trigger, but it does not go off and is additionally armed with a machete and numerous knives? The madman was violently resisting arrest and assaulting the officer in the process.

Martin clearly should have been nominated by his senior officers for the highest gallantry award. That was overlooked and it was not the arresting officer that was overzealous but his senior officers in suspending him for 6 months. During which time they should have been investigated for neglect of duty for failing to recommend the brave officer for his well-earned gallantry medal award.

The error is glaringly obvious and corroborated by the awarding of a belated, by 21 years, mere chief constable's award.

Who has ever heard of a chief constable commending an officer 21 years after the incident? No one I'll bet!

Martin was given that as a token gesture and afterthought by a thoughtful Chief Constable Thompson. It was not he who had blundered. He was just left to pick up the pieces and offer a weak apology. The culprit chief constable had long since retired and no doubt with his knighthood medal.

The time eligibility period for nominations of gallantry awards had expired and so Martin was robbed of his recognition. (The National Awards Advisory Group will usually only consider award nominations submitted within 12-18 months of the incident/issue.)

Martin, sir, you are the true gallant knight in this embarrassingly cringe worthy tale. You were cheated out of your gallantry recognition and again of a LS & GC medal by your severe injury.

He left the service without any form of medal to even show any connection to the police... BUT this is not over yet because I do not want him and others to wait another 21 years before the failings are accepted!

I have added a comprehensive list of Martin's police service injuries. It makes for harrowing reading but is enlightening as to the dangers faced by officers daily in the UK.

Can anyone hand on heart say the campaign is not needed and that members of the so-called 'police family' do not fail their own?

Malcolm Murphy

Malcolm Murphy

I joined the Greater Manchester Police Force in 1977 and I was medically discharged in 1999.

My injuries happened because the police van, I was driving was ambushed by youths who threw bricks and concrete through the windscreen of the police vehicle. I had to make very sharp manoeuvres in attempting to avoid the continuing attack and in doing so somehow damaged my left knee and right hip joint. I think that was the start of my PTSD.

It was sometime in 1998, when I was in a police van accompanied by another officer, and it was about 1am. We were patrolling Leigh subdivision and specifically the Kirkhall Road area of the town.

As we drove along that road we were suddenly hit by a barrage of bricks and lumps of concrete, some coming through the windscreen and a vehicle then started driving at us at speed and further missiles were thrown.

I was driving the van and started making sharp manoeuvres to try and avoid the attacking vehicle. This went on for several minutes and we were radioing for assistance.

I eventually drove onto the pavement and towards the offending vehicle which was on the footway aiming towards us. I believed that attack was our best form of defence and I aimed for it intending to ram it. However, the vehicle veered off and disappeared.

By this time assistance had arrived and back at the station I was aching from the body movements I had made to avoid the attacking vehicle.

The officer in charge attended and enquired about the incident and offered me counselling. I declined as I didn't think I would need it. I carried on with my tour of duty. Later it became clear I was suffering from PTSD.

Several weeks later I was the subject of an attack by a female whilst I arrested her. My shirt was torn, and I received several smacks.

I didn't go off sick, but I think the accumulation of the attacks got to me and I think I started suffering from PTSD. I didn't want to go to work and worried about anything and everything.

During the initial attack I'd discovered that I'd injured my left knee and right hip. Over time the injuries got progressively worse, and I was attending the hospital for medical treatment.

I subsequently had 2 knee joint scrapes followed by a complete knee replacement. I also had several consultations and x-rays on my right hip and then a full hip replacement. These were sometime after the incidents as I was determined to carry on. However, it beat me in the end. I was happy that I did manage to complete over 22 years and received my 'Long Service and Good Conduct Medal'. I received no welfare or care from the police, and I was eventually medically discharged with a lower rate injury pension.

Author's comment.

Malcolm only had his PTSD recognised by the police, but he also had his physical injuries too. He was fortunate enough to receive his LS & GC medal and so, unlike many, he does have something to show a connection to the Police Service.

However, my view is that he should also receive the medal I propose. I note he received no welfare care from within the police.

Tom Curry

Tom Curry

My own story

I am proud to be the son of a Northumbrian coal miner. I was the first one for generations not to follow the family tradition to enter the coal mining industry.

I joined the West Sussex Constabulary as a cadet in September 1967. In 1968 I was sworn in as a constable with the then amalgamated Sussex Police. From then on, I never wanted to be anything but a proactive police constable and to be 'on the streets' with the public.

I gained 6 Chief Constable's Commendations. One of those I was recommended for a Queen's Police Medal by my inspector, but it was not supported by our renowned serial womanising and drunkard of a superintendent.

This man took a disliking to me whilst taking a liking to my 19-year-old girlfriend, irrespective of the fact that he was in his early 50s, even asking her for a date on several occasions but was declined.

That is sufficient information to indicate perhaps the reason for him not supporting my inspector's nomination.

I will give the details of the incident only to show how police can be called upon to protect the public whilst risking their own safety and for one reason or another can be deprived of deserved medal recognition, as I was together with my young colleague.

On the 11th of August 1982, I was single crewed in a marked police car, when I was sent to a man going berserk during a domestic dispute. On the way and on seeing a young probationer, PC Gary Tutt, I took it upon myself to pick him up and take him along. When we got to the address, we found that a man had smashed his mother's lovely home to pieces. She had run from the house to escape his violent attack. Gary and I went to the front door, and it was immediately thrown open. The man rushed at us, pointing a loaded, high-powered by gas, diver's spear gun.

There was little time, but I managed to jump aside and grab the spear gun, whilst endeavouring to keep it pointed away from us, as we struggled violently to contain him. The man still holding the spear gun grabbed Gary's somewhat heavy personal radio from its harness and smashed him over the head with it.

Gary was knocked unconscious and collapsed. I continued to struggle with the man on the ground and during this time, I spotted the leather strap of Gary's truncheon sticking out from his pocket. I grabbed it and heaved it out, all the time holding on to the spear gun and struggling with the man. In a split second, I had the truncheon and I belted him with it, straight on the top of his head as hard as I could. I had now knocked him out. Gary came around and we cuffed the man behind his back. We searched him and found he had two lethal-looking diving daggers hidden on him. One was tucked in the belt of his trousers and the other was strapped to his lower leg. The man was gushing blood, and we were all covered.

After he came around, we took him to the car and bandaged his head to try and stem the blood. Other officers arrived and we were happy to hand him over, whilst Gary and I recovered. The man who was covered in blood had not said anything up to now, but I will never forget what he did say. He looked straight at me and said, and I promise this is word for word exactly, "I'll tell you what, you've ruined my day." Phew! I'll tell you what, he got very close to ruining ours!

His mother was extremely grateful to us. The man needed stitches. Gary had a bump the size of an egg on his head, but no stitches were required.

Our section inspector did a report to the Chief Constable recommending both of us to be honoured with a Queen's Police Medal. His direct boss, the superintendent, endorsed the report that he did not agree, and the poor, well-meaning inspector was told he should not have made the recommendation. Without the superintendent's endorsement, the award of the QPM award was not going to happen, and it did not.

The inspector went on to become a deputy chief constable thus overtaking the rank of the superintendent and so his opinion was likely to be credible.

As consolation we were both given a Chief Constable's Commendation, for the 'courage and tenacity we displayed in disarming and arresting the disturbed man, who was subsequently not charged with any offence but was committed to a psychiatric hospital'.

We were both robbed of a gallantry medal which we had deservedly earned but that was not to be the only medal I was narrowly to miss out on.

This story is included because although I was not injured, my young colleague was, and it perfectly illustrates the everyday extreme dangers officers can face. It is also appropriate because it is another example of how officers can be deprived of a gallantry medal, as was Martin Gill too, and only because a senior officer either cannot be bothered to make the nomination or the potential recipient's 'face does not fit'.

I was injured on countless occasions including being stabbed in the head, 2 back injuries necessitating hospitalisation and on one occasion when pursuing jewellery shop robbers, shots were fired but I escaped injury.

In 1989 I attended a nightclub when my young probationer colleague and I were viciously attacked by a drunken mob. He was knocked unconscious, and I was violently and repeatedly kicked in the neck and back as I lay on the ground still wrestling with the ringleader.

I sustained life-changing neck and back injuries which gradually became worse and triggered a complaint, not widely known, being that of 'ankylosing spondylitis' and exacerbated by the attack.

After about a year off sick and repeated attempts to return to work, I was forced out of the job I loved and medically discharged from the service.

I was very ill in the beginning until my complaints were properly clinically diagnosed and I received the appropriate treatment and medication.

At first a few colleagues visited me at home during the year I was off sick but quite quickly the visits became almost nil. It was noticeable that no one visited me in their own time and when not on duty. Those who did were fond of a wee dram or two. Yes, on duty and in uniform and driving a marked police vehicle but anything I provided was in moderation. Although I do confess as the provider, I did condone it. I told you I'd tell the truth at the start!

I recall on one rare visit from one of my sergeants, I was expressing my worries for the future and of having to leave the job I loved. I heard a non-speaking noise coming from his direction. It stopped me in mid-sentence because there was little point of continuing with my woes, because the noise I heard coming from my sergeant, who had earlier expressed his concern for my welfare, was that of... snoring!

From start to finish, I received no support from either the Police Federation or the welfare officer. The one and only time the force welfare officer visited me was when he came to serve the official papers for my medical discharge.

Once he'd completed that, I now relate word for word our final exchange. The retired former detective chief superintendent, then a civilian but still employed by Sussex Police in the role as force welfare officer said, "There is only one further thing to arrange and that is for you to see the Chief Constable for him to wish you farewell, when will that be convenient?"

At that stage having been semi-paralysed, mainly by the pain, but still retaining my somewhat cynical sense of humour, I replied, "Anytime really, I'm in most days!" He looked surprised and said, "Oh! It would mean that you will have to go to police HQ to see him." I said, "That hardly seems fair, the Chief having access to the force helicopter and me being unwell." After a pause and looking at me oddly, he said, "What do you want to do then?" I said, "The only option is we had better leave it then." At that he left.

I had already decided I would not be attending any farcical 'farewell from the Chief' appointment. This was greatly influenced by a story related to me in the 70s, when I was very young in service.

I was in the CID office one afternoon when a retiring detective constable returned from his visit to the Chief Constable. The detective's name was Jack (Nobby) Clark. Nobby said, "What a farce! The Chief had to keep looking down at a note on his desk to remember my name and soon ran out of things to say."

Back then, the Chief gave a retirement gift (joke!) of either a paperweight or small wooden wall shield, both with the force emblem on them. (I got nothing!)

The Chief said to Nobby, "What would you like a paperweight or a wall shield?" Nobby said, "A paperweight please." The Chief from his desk spoke on his intercom to his secretary saying, "Mr Clark will have a paperweight." A few moments later his intercom sounded, and a voice said, "We haven't got any paperweights left, will he have a wall shield?" The Chief looked at Nobby who nodded in agreement.

Nobby added, in exasperation, "30 years in the job and you still don't get what you want but get what you're given. He didn't even offer to get a paperweight and send it to me!" and threw the shield onto his desk.

I think that sums it up and I never forgot the tale. I ensured I avoided the Chief's farewell.

So, when I was able to, I put all my uniforms and accessories into bin bags and one Saturday morning I delivered them to the police station. I'd been off sick a year and had handed back my warrant card. The member of staff on the public counter was new and did not know me. A serving officer who had been there sometime was found and identified me. I was let into the police station, and I went to the general office placed the bags on the floor and went home after 23 ½ years of service.

The only thing I own to show any connection to the Police Service is a piece of paper that says, 'Sussex Police. This certificate is presented to

Thomas William Curry upon his retirement in sincere appreciation and recognition of service as a police officer'. Signed by Roger Birch, Chief Constable, dated 8 December 1989. On the rear it states my conduct was 'exemplary'.

At that time, the eligibility for the LS & GC Medal was 22 years, which I came so VERY close to but ONLY through the injury did not receive it. Guess how close I got?... 6 weeks!

I had been connected to the Police Service for over 23 years for I had been a cadet BUT that extra year + did not count.

So, there was to be no medal for me.

I do not even compare the severity of my injuries with the plight of my friends confined to wheelchairs and in many cases with brain damage. As bad as mine are, I think I was lucky to escape their harrowing fate.

This campaign I assure you is not about me, even in the slightest degree, and if an award is approved retrospectively after 34 years, only when forced by myself and after such a lengthy time-lapse, I would be tempted to say, 'I suggest it might be prudent to cover it in grease to ease insertion!'

However, I would appear gracious in acceptance but only because it will prevent those, who sadly will be injured in the future, from feeling the same as I/we did i.e. disillusionment, saddened, dejected, overlooked and worthless!

One can only feel sorrow when a seasoned and dedicated copper at the top of his game loses the job he loved and lived for (absolutely true) and is treated in such a cavalier manner. This is especially true when the attacker was sentenced to only 100 hours of community service BUT that's another matter!

Foolishly some may say, I learned nothing from my injury experience to stop me getting involved in situations which others shy away from and the following story depicts just that.

In 2014, at the age of 65 years, 25 years after being medically discharged from the police and still carrying my injuries, I witnessed a group of youths fighting in Hastings town centre. One of them produced a 13" carving knife and ran amok chasing the others. Although it was daylight and very busy, no one made a move to intervene except me. He dumped the knife in a waste bin, which I recovered. I saw him remove his coat and run off. Ahh! I thought, our boy's been nicked before and is conscious of being identified on description. A slight change in his dress might fool an amateur and less competent witness but not me.

About 20 minutes later, a long way from the scene and in company with a uniform cop, I identified him. He said looking at my shorts and perhaps my grey hair, "Who are you? You ain't a copper."

I said, "No, I'm not but I'm still the guy who's going to get you locked up!"

I was the only witness as no one else came forward, including those who were involved and chased.

The next day, he only got a 26-week custodial sentence and for the serious matter of running wild with a huge knife in broad daylight in a busy town centre.

I received no thanks from anyone, including the police but that will still not deter me. Why don't I just mind my own business? It's simple, I was once a cop, and it looks like I'm always going to think like a cop! (Retired)... And maybe I just like to keep my hand in. I really must try to get out a bit more!

Years later and as a result of a lovely lady in Northern Ireland, then unknown to me, after merely reading my autobiography and being impressed by what I became, my exploits and charitable work, she researched me further and nominated me for a 'British Citizen Award'. I received the recognition on 14 January 2022.

The certificate reads:

Certificate of Recognition. 'This is to certify that Thomas Curry has been recognised by The British Citizen Award for his exceptional contribution to society and being an inspiration to other British Citizens.'

I tell folks that it is only a minor award, but Prince Andrew would like it to replace all his 'honorary' medals that were swiftly snatched back!

More than I ever got from the police, eh?

Regarding the frequent quote:

'The Thin Blue Line and those who run towards danger instead of away, are valued.'

I don't think so. I have yet to see any real evidence of that other than patronising propaganda and rhetoric claptrap!

I, along with many injured others, left the Police Service without any medal whatsoever to even show a connection, ADDING INSULT TO INJURY!

(However, the Sussex Police were not satisfied just to leave it at that, as you will read further on in Chapter 6. The Skulduggery of The Sussex Police Pensions' Authority.)

Dave Stamp

I served with the Sussex Police from 1971 to 2001. I knew and worked with the author, Tom Curry, in the 80s at Worthing police station. I can remember two incidents when he sustained back injuries and then after the third it resulted in him being medically discharged.

I did my thirty years and finished my time at Brighton as a sergeant. The last couple of years I had served as a custody sergeant when things were a lot tougher than today and in very difficult working conditions. I guess somebody didn't like me but luckily, we had good staff, and a sense of humour always helps.

I was assaulted very early in my service whilst at Hove in the 70's and the offending female got three months straight off with no messing and it wasn't a serious assault.

Other similar incidents resulted in my losing a couple of teeth. The loss took a time as the blood supply had been cut off to the teeth. I applied for and eventually received a Criminal Injuries' Compensation payment.

I did receive a LS & GC Medal, which I must confess I didn't value very much at the time until Tom's campaign brought the unfairness of those discharged prior to their completion of 22 years' service struck me.

When I ponder things, I can think of quite a number of colleagues who never made it to 22 years. I've never had occasion to wear the medal and I think the only time it has been out of its box is when a friend had lost his and had to attend a formal function with the Sheriff and I lent him mine.

I am increasingly aware of officers receiving injuries at various stages of service which result in their discharge. I believe in luck and a police officer's luck can change in an instant more than most people. I don't think there is currently a system acknowledging those who don't make the 22 years (now 20 years) contribution to the public good. A medal would mean something to a lot of people.

Author's comment.

Happily, my friend, Dave, was able to complete his full 30 years' service. I have included his contribution because it comes from the perspective of one who did receive his LS & GC Medal and was fortunate enough not to be medically discharged but witnessed many who were.

PC Nick Lindsay

PC Nick Lindsay

My name is Nick Lindsay, and I was born in 1970. I joined the Metropolitan Police Service in 2002 and I am still serving.

On the 8th of August 2011, I was posted on a Safer Neighbourhood's Team within the Croydon Borough. My colleague and I were on duty the night it kicked off in Tottenham after the police shooting of Mark Duggan. In the light of the events, we were tasked to patrol Croydon town centre, as intelligence suggested that Croydon was going to see a rise in public disorder, like many other areas across London.

We patrolled and engaged with groups of youths, in what was a very tense atmosphere across the town centre. We were then told to man cordons at the West Croydon end of the town centre. It was here that I saw several buses abandoned in the road with smashed windows and a large crowd of people approaching us, clearly with criminal intent, as they took up the whole road. At this point there were approximately 20 police officers in standard beat uniform covering this end of town. Our own public order trained officers had been deployed to Greenwich.

We then started to receive missiles of various sizes being thrown in our own direction and could see looting occurring in shops further down the road.

We were eventually provided with short shields. These had been collected from every station across the borough. However, several shields broke under the onslaught of missiles we were receiving. As the mass of rioters got to within 20 to 30 feet from our rather extended line, covering 5 junctions, it was evident that we were in a precarious situation. It was at this point I noticed a group attacking someone in the mass of people; it was soon after that I caught glimpses of a police community support officer's (PCSO) uniform worn by the person on the floor and who was getting seriously assaulted.

I ran into the crowd, followed by 4 officers, hitting anyone who blocked our passage with my baton. We grabbed the PCSO off the floor and managed to get him back inside of our cordon. He had several head wounds and needed surgery to his eye later that night. For this action I was awarded a deputy commissioner's commendation but almost 2 years after the event.

We returned to our line and moved into Tamworth Road. Six of us covered that cordon line, but only after we moved two abandoned buses into the road to close off one lane. Whilst we covered that road junction, we could see another bus had been set alight and Reeves Corner furniture store was well and truly ablaze.

It was here that shouts from other police lines alerted us to a car that had driven at speed through the police line on London Road. It turned in our direction and we all had our backs to the oncoming threat as we had a large mass or rioters approaching us. It was only the noise of screeching tyres and racing engine, that made us break for cover. I caught a glancing blow from the speeding car and was thrown to the side of the road. Thankfully, I only received heavy bruising to my side, mainly from the impact and being thrown to the side of the road. Adrenaline obviously played a part in my quick recovery and getting back to blocking the road with my colleagues.

This was an event that was the catalyst for my future diagnoses of PTSD.

My deterioration occurred shortly after the disorder, my anger management became worse, especially towards those I worked alongside. This was so much so that I received a complaint from a colleague. My family also took a lot of my frustration and anger, which was not fair on them, but I didn't see the issue. I was OK as far as I thought.

It was during this tenure that I was informed of a credible threat to the life of my family and myself. The suspect is still outstanding for a hit and run death within the Borough.

This all compounded the moral injury, later to be known as Post Traumatic Stress Disorder.

Whilst on response I attended numerous calls where lawful force had to be applied to effect arrest, and I was punched and kicked at a number of these calls.

I was first on scene at a child death. Being a father myself it was a difficult call.

I was also assaulted by a youth, who was muscular, as he boxed and played rugby. He was assaulting a teacher and I intervened. He got me in a choke hold and was trying to strangle me, but I managed to get the better of him and he was arrested for assault on police.

I became a recluse being too afraid to go out and I hated being cooped up at home. I was agoraphobic and my old PTSD stuff became a recurring theme. I couldn't handle crowded places and shopping trips to the supermarket were joyless for my wife. She frequently witnessed me have an anxiety attack and sprint around the shop only to leave the full trolley at the till queue because it wasn't going quick enough for me.

Many times, I had to rush out of the store before I broke down or ended up losing it and hitting someone. I eventually went back to work, as I was at the point of half pay, and would be in financial hardship if that occurred.

I was part of the Grenfell Tower body recovery efforts, spending time at the scene recovering the remains of victims.

I made an attempt to take my own life. I had become so disillusioned with the job, its lack of duty of care and empathy. I saw no way of making the persistent negativity stop, the only way was to end my life. Not my finest hour, I still have suicidal ideations daily but now manage not to act on them.

So, I find myself currently, off sick with no further treatment options. I can no longer enter a police force building without having an anxiety attack and I face going on half pay next month. I have no trust in senior management whatsoever. I have had no contact from colleagues from my old team. A lesson learned is that job friends they are not. They are just colleagues who you work with.

I used to enjoy being a police officer and I held the position operationally for 20 years. It's only for the last 2 years or so that I have been restricted to the point of being fully office based and in non-public facing roles. I had pride in what I did and helping people who needed my help was my vocation in life. I didn't join to get injured on duty or become ill due to the rigours of policing.

My family did not expect to have to deal with my extreme mood swings, deep bouts of depression, an attempt on my life and poor anger management. I no longer have pride in the job, or myself. I am broken through policing.

Author's comment.

I think everyone should read Nick's tale, whether they suffer from PTSD or not.

He graphically explains the problems encountered by modern-day frontline police officers in these turbulent times, the terrible effects of PTSD and most of all the lack of care and compassion from the 'police family' for their very own.

I am so pleased I have decided to put this book together to document and highlight both the injuries sustained and the failings within the Police Service to take proper care of those who need it most.

I believe this inclusion alone highlights not only the flaws in police welfare but also in the Police Federation's duty to represent their members and to fight on their behalf to get the best possible support and outcome in such cases.

I am grateful to Nick for sharing the details of his brave acts, at a worrying time for both him and his family too, and for having the true courage to relive them again in contributing to this book. In doing so I am confident it will be of benefit to many readers in their understanding of the complexities and struggles with PTSD.

Stephen Finegold

Stephen Finegold

I joined the Metropolitan Police Cadet Corps in September 1975 and was attested as a constable at Hendon Training Centre on 19th December 1977. In 1983 I was promoted to sergeant and transferred to Bow Street police station before serving as Officer in Charge of the Divisional Information and Intelligence Unit at Bethnal Green police station.

One evening in April 1987 I attended the scene of a burglary in progress at premises in Bethnal Green Road. I spotted a suspect on the roof of the premises and climbed a wall and lower roof to gain access to the upper roof where the suspect had been seen. I shouted for the suspect to stop and tried to reach out to him, but he swung away from me and then appeared to fall through the roof and at the same time I lost my footing and slid off the roof.

I landed on a pile of what appeared to be scrap metal around twenty feet below the roof. I realised I had been badly injured with severe pain to my legs and back and that I needed help quickly. I radioed the station but had to wait a considerable time to be found. After being recovered and carried to a local cafe to await an ambulance I could see that my leg was at an odd angle and that the pain in my back was becoming worse. An ambulance arrived and I was taken to the accident and emergency room at the Royal London Hospital.

The doctors ordered an x-ray on my leg but despite my complaining of back pain this was not investigated or examined. I was told of a fracture to my leg and sent home on crutches.

At the time I was living with my fiancée, and she was able to care for me, as I rested in bed, while at the same time she was also travelling daily to her workplace. After a few days, I noticed my back was increasing in pain and woke one morning terrified that I was unable to move my legs and had been incontinent. I was able to call my doctor and she attended and advised me to stay as still as possible and she would send an ambulance. Her examination concluded I had a possible fracture of the spine. I was eventually taken to a local A&E where my spine was x-rayed which showed that I had two fractures, one in the lower thoracic region and one in the lumber region.

I was admitted to a ward and put on complete bed rest for 8 weeks. I was told I may not be able to walk again. It appears that after the fall the first hospital missed the fractures in my back and my movement at home caused haemorrhaging leading to compression and scar tissue on my spinal cord. Some feeling and some movement returned to my legs over time, and I was discharged in a wheelchair. I was admitted to the Metropolitan Police Nursing home in Hendon where I stayed for around 6 months. During this time, I received very little help or visits from my colleagues apart from one friend who was able to help get my fiancée to visit me in Hendon and to give me a lift home on a few weekends' leave before returning me to the nursing home.

Around a year after the injury on duty I was medically discharged from the force. I had to wear a device on my right leg which allowed me to walk with assistance and essentially, I had to re-learn how to walk. The force showed no interest in my welfare after this time and in fact, decided to re-assess my injury award after a few years and reduced it arguing that I had clearly improved in my ability to walk. In fact, the symptoms were exactly the same. I have had no contact from any senior officers since my medical discharge.

My fiancée who was by now my wife was instrumental in my continuing care. As we were not married at the time of my accident, although we were living together and engaged to be married, she will not be entitled to a full widow's pension when I die. This is an awful situation for her, the one person who cared for me after the IOD.

I can manage without a wheelchair now, but I am still unable to feel my feet and right leg. I have multiple mobility issues and suffer from continuous pain from the fracture sites and associated neurological complications.

Author's comment.

Poor Stephen's life changed forever after his fall from the roof. He states, like so many others, that he received no after care from the Police Service.

He fully deserves a medal to show he was a police officer and his enormous health sacrifice.

Pennie Payne

Sir John Stevens Met. Commissioner presenting Pennie with her 'Certificate of Service' accompanied by her husband, Darryl.

Darryl Payne and his wife, Pennie were both police officers in the Metropolitan Police. Darryl served from 1983-2009. Pennie served from 1993 until 2002, when she was medically discharged because of her catastrophic injury on duty.

The following piece is written by Darryl on behalf of Pennie:

It was New Year's Eve 1994 when Pennie and a colleague were called to identify the driver of a vehicle who was believed to be disqualified from driving.

On arrival at the scene, she was instructed to stay with the driver's girlfriend while the driver was arrested. During the arrest, the driver put up a violent struggle which caused the girlfriend to become animated and angry. Pennie tried to calm the girlfriend down but to no avail and she went berserk hitting Pennie on the head 4 times with a lump of metal she had in her clutch bag knocking her unconscious. She then struck another male officer breaking his nose.

Pennie woke up after a short time, but no ambulance was called to the scene for her. Pennie went back to the station to write up her evidence and later noted that her writing was like that of a 5-year-old, a clear indication that she was suffering from concussion. A chance interaction with a doctor present at the station on another matter saw him insist she was taken directly to hospital as he noted her pupils were unequal and fixed, a sign that something was very wrong.

Pennie spent the rest of the night and the next day at Newham General Hospital where she was monitored but did not receive a computed tomography (CT) scan.

Over the next day or two her condition worsened considerably, and she was taken to a local hospital. There they scanned her and discovered a catastrophic bleed on her brain. Under police escort, with blue lights, she was transferred to St Bartholomew's Hospital neurosurgical unit in central London where they operated on her.

During the operation she 'died' twice but was resuscitated and due to the damage that a brain haemorrhage had done to one of the ventricles of her brain she had a ventricular peritoneal (VP) shunt permanently inserted into her brain. This in simple terms is an internal pumping system to re-circulate cerebral spinal fluid from the fourth ventricle of the brain back into the body as the brain was no longer able to perform this function itself.

Although critical for a few days she eventually stabilised. While she was in intensive care only one senior officer visited her and then only because he happened to be at the Old Bailey around the corner that day giving evidence.

Pennie was off sick for 8 months during which time she had to learn to both walk and talk again. Her rehabilitation was slow and difficult and during that time she had very little contact from the Met. Police, no contact from her police team and no support other than from her own parents and was nursed back to health by her mother.

Eight months later Pennie finally returned to full duty, refusing the offer to be medically retired by the Chief Medical Officer. She was the first and only fully operational police officer with a VP shunt in the world.

Through her own determination she was to remain fully operational for another seven years, but the road was a rocky one as she battled malfunction and failures of the shunt, each setback requiring further major brain surgery. During those years she spent time at both Romford and West End Central.

Between 1995 and 2002, Pennie underwent over ten major brain surgeries struggling back to full duty through grit, determination and a burning desire to fulfil her life's dream of being a police officer. Recuperation time was spent in CID offices and the West End licensing office but as soon as she was fit and her hair had grown back, she returned to full operational street duties.

With every operation however, it was becoming clear to her that the patience of police senior management was wearing thin, and she was fast being seen as 'a problem'.

In early 2002, Pennie was told that 'risk assessments had changed and that she would no longer be able to remain operational'. A fight through the Federation to stay operational failed to gain traction. Finally, during a visit to the Chief Medical Officer she was medically retired, and his words were, 'For you, soldier, the war is over'. Those words were the last thing she ever wanted to hear, and it affected her very badly. Problems with her memory and neurological functioning meant that she was classed as 78% permanently disabled.

Within days of her medical retirement her inspector attended

Pennie's home with a prisoner's property bag containing just a few personal effects, the last sad evidence of a stolen career. Human Resources and senior managers had emptied her locker in her absence and without informing her, had disposed of everything except her personal property. Even the police hat bearing the scars of that night's assault, a daily reminder each time she went to her locker at the start of a shift of how lucky she was to be alive, had been unceremoniously discarded.

Her certificate of service was posted to her in the mail. There was no exit interview, no, thank you for your service, no sorry this happened. Nothing! She felt unwanted, unappreciated, and thrown to the kerbside like rubbish.

A while later I happened to meet Sir John Stevens when he was The Met. Commissioner, I told him Pennie's story and he agreed to present her certificate to her in retrospect at his office at New Scotland Yard, a nice gesture but this was more due to the character of the great man himself than the organisation he represented. This would never have happened without my intervention and certainly never occurred to Pennie's own police managers. They did, however, make sure their station was represented by one of their inspectors on the day!

In the years since that first incident Pennie has undergone 18 major brain surgeries, 'died' twice more and been found in a coma by me in the morning more than once.

Pennie is permanently disabled, has lost 40% of her vision and we have two children from 9 pregnancies, the miscarriages being caused by her condition and the presence of the shunt drainage tube.

Both of our surviving children were born prematurely our son 10 weeks early, still born but resuscitated and our daughter 13 weeks early weighing less than 1lb and profoundly deaf from birth because of complications arising from her prematurity.

On a happier side note our son is now 24 and at medical school studying to be an anaesthesiologist in Alabama. Our daughter, who despite being profoundly deaf is pitch perfect, a straight A student in her second year at university in Florida studying criminology and criminal psychology on a path to work for the FBI.

To this day Pennie suffers from low self-esteem, severe PTSD alongside physical pain but never complains. She and I are immensely disappointed with the job and the way she was treated and that was one of the driving factors for us leaving the UK. Seeing police cars driving past was a constant and painful reminder of the career she lost after such a short period of time, a career that held so much potential as Pennie entered the service as a bright, driven individual on the accelerated promotion scheme being a university graduate with a degree in sociology and a Russian speaker.

The failings of the police management did not end there. Around 2006 Pennie was in intensive care in the Neuro unit in London with a shunt failure and septicaemia caused by an infection in the tubing in her abdomen, the remnants of several previous operations. By then our 6-year-old son and 2-year-old handicapped daughter, at this time still oxygen dependent, were with me 70 miles from the hospital. I was running from Canterbury to London and back every day juggling to spin the plates as carer, husband, father and home keeper.

After just 2 weeks' compassionate leave I was told by my own senior management team that I had to return to work. I was the sergeant of a Safer Neighbourhood Team at the time and the role was being more than capably managed by an acting police sergeant.

Both I and the Federation representative pled my case, but we were told that the solution was for me to employ a full-time nanny, a little difficult on a sergeant's wage! The meeting ended badly with me throwing my warrant card at the Chief Inspector and walking out. That's how much the job cares about the welfare of their officers and especially one that had quite literally given everything and almost her life for. I was done!

Skilful bridge building by the Federation representative, a cool head when the dust settled, I re-thought my career options and decided to remain long enough to collect a reasonable pension, this was to be the key to leaving the country and a new start for a brave but unappreciated lady. I retired in 2009 and we now live in the USA.

Author's comment.

I find myself struggling to find the words to explain the deep sadness I feel on hearing the tragic story of poor Pennie. I also feel an equal amount of anger towards the system which let both her and husband, Darryl, down so badly.

Although, it is over 20 years ago, Pennie continues to suffer every day. The only consolation is that she is fortunately supported by her devoted husband.

Pennie is a prime candidate for my medal proposal. I am fully aware that it will not make her life any more bearable, but it will give the long overdue recognition she earned back in 2002.

Mark Humphreys

Mark Humphreys

In 2009 I was a Metropolitan police constable at Heathrow Airport with 26 years' service. My wife was very ill and other things had happened at home that I don't want to disclose.

It was on 6 September 2009 at about 1700 hrs., and I was driving a response car when a call came that someone had fallen from a great height onto concrete at the airport. We answered the call to block the area off for the air ambulance and set off on 'blues and two's' (blue lights and sirens) on the A4.

As I rounded the corner on the dual carriageway doing about 70mph a young boy on a push bike rode straight out in front of me. I swerved to avoid him and, in that instance, put myself and my colleague into the crash barrier. I looked in the mirror and the boy and bike were lying in the middle of the road.

At first, we couldn't get out of the damaged car, but my partner kicked his door open, and we ran back. The boy was bleeding somewhere from his face and just kept saying, "It's my fault I didn't see you." I looked at him and I imagined my own son dying in the road.

Everyone arrived and they took me away to the nick, I was breathalysed, drug tested and had my firearms taken from me. I was interviewed by a traffic sergeant, then told I could go home. I was in tears and couldn't face any of my colleagues and friends. The night duty officers drove me home and that was it. I had spent my life protecting people and now I thought I had killed a kid.

A few hours later I received a call that he had survived but the damage was done, as far as I was concerned, I thought I'd killed him but to this day I don't even remember hitting him. This was the start, and I had a complete breakdown.

I hid in the house, wouldn't open the door or answer the phone. I was put on all kinds of drugs to keep me calm from outbursts of anger, depression and violent mood swings. My sergeant came around and took my firearms' permit from me in case I took out a firearm, but I never went back. In one and a half years not one supervisor came to see me.

I saw the Chief Medical Officer (CMO) a couple of times and was bounced all over the place from doctor to psychiatrist but what a waste of time that was. I was a complete wreck I would get lost going to the supermarket. I rang my wife one day when I was going to Tesco's in Teddington but had found myself heading down the M3.

The alcohol was my escape and obviously my marriage and family suffered terribly. Eventually a new chief inspector arrived at the station and asked, "Who is this Mark Humphreys shown as one of my officers and where is he?" A meeting was organised with me and my wife. "Who is looking after this officer?" the Chief Inspector asked.

Human Resources (HR) thought Personnel, they thought the inspector and the inspector thought the sergeant was. No one was and for almost two years.

I went to see the CMO again and whilst waiting the secretary called him and said, "Your 10 o'clock is here." My wife, Federation representative and I went through, and he didn't even look up and just started going through his tick list.

He got to, "Have you ever thought of self-harm?" I said, "Yes. I am going to drive down to the Thames at Hampton Court and park my car and leave the engine running and the hazard lights on so it can be found. I'm going to wear my fluorescent jacket and go into the river so drunk that I won't care and weigh myself down. I will wear my police jacket so the body will be found quickly, and the ambulance crew or police won't have to drag out a rotting body after a few weeks. I will be dead so that will end it all quickly and nobody will wonder if I'm alive or not. My name is Mark Humphreys, I'm not just your 10 o'clock!"

That was it all hell broke loose, and my wife was in tears. The Federation representative was in shock and the CMO was in a panic. The Met. got rid of me as fast as possible. I hit the drink big time until last year when I was offered a job in Malta where I'm now living. My family is still in the UK because my wife wouldn't put up with the drinking anymore.

There is a lot more, I was helped by mates in the Army and Veterans' Associations as the police didn't help PTSD sufferers. All of this came from a car accident that was my last straw.

I joined The Met. 15 August 1983, and my official retirement date was 8 September 2012. During that time, I went through riots, bombings, bodies, domestics, suicides the lot and this was my last day as a police officer.

I had it all and lost it all. As I write this, I'm still sitting in tears all this time later.

Author's comment.

This sad tale began on the day of the accident, something that could have happened to any one of us.

It's a disgrace that Mark had to seek help outside of the police from the Army Veterans' Association. Doesn't that say it all?

Grant Prescott

Grant Prescott

My name is Grant Prescott, and I joined the Metropolitan Police on 15th September 1979, and I served until 1989 when I transferred to North Yorkshire Police and became a motorcycle traffic officer.

On 16 December 1998, I attended a serious road traffic accident on 'blues and two's'. There was another police car about 100 metres ahead of me as we passed stationary vehicles on the A59 Harrogate to York Road and at Cattall a car attempted a U turn without looking and pulled out straight across my path.

My speed was about 70mph and as soon as the bike hit the car, I was catapulted some 43 metres where I lost consciousness. I came to and could not feel my legs. I panicked and screamed in shock. I was eventually taken into hospital and slowly feeling came back to my legs, but my left side did not work properly, and I was in constant agony. I spent some time in a wheelchair when the pain was too much.

My immediate colleagues visited regularly but no senior officers. I was in and out of hospital where eventually they ascertained what was causing the pain, I have nerve damage at the base of my spine and across the left side and down the left leg.

After the crash I eventually returned home but I was not able to return to work.

It was about a year later when I was called to see the force medical officer, and I was told that I was being medically retired. I was a tad upset and saw him again a few weeks later when he told me I was medically retired and the level I would be retired on was 4, the highest one. My official retirement date was 27 December 1999.

It all didn't make much sense to me until I saw a Federation representative and he explained it all and basically said, "That's it, you're done."

All I got was countless letters regarding medical retirement but no acknowledgement from a senior staff member, no thanks for your service, just official retirement letters.

I have had so many surgical procedures that I have lost count how many they total. The latest was 16 September 2023 here in New Zealand. As the pain is constant, I have a spinal cord stimulator in my body, basically an internal tens machine which is to mask the pain. Some days it's no good at all even with strong medication. Night-time is worse, and I'm deprived of sleep.

What irked me the most was I never did receive my 'Long Service and Good Conduct Medal' entitlement and they didn't even write a letter acknowledging my 20 years 3 months' great service.

A medal to display to recognise I had a connection to the Police Service and was injured on duty would be appreciated.

Author's comment.

Yet another case of no care received and no medal. (Eligibility for LS & GC Medal was 22 years during Grant's service period.)

John Smith

John Smith

My Story, John Smith, 19 years' police service 1975-1994, Police Cadet, Police Constable, Police Sergeant.

A little bit of background:

I was badly injured on duty whilst making an arrest on New Year's Eve in 1988 in Blackpool town centre. Initially I soon returned to full operational police duty. I had been injured many times before during my operational police career. Each one while confronting violent offenders and subsequently detaining them until assistance arrived.

However, the injuries sustained on New Year's Eve 1988 were far more significant than I initially realised. They did not resolve and continued to worsen.

That night I was acting police sergeant, driving a Transit Personnel

Carrier with a team of regulars and special constables onboard in Blackpool. At the earlier briefing, we were provided with a response role to attend assistance shouts and 999 calls where assaults or significant public disorder were in progress.

Around 5 to midnight, I'd parked us up in the town centre, just a short hop away from where the main celebrations were going to be as New Year struck. A minute or so later we heard over the radio that a PC was in pursuit of a man on foot who had become violent towards the officer as he was attempting to detain him for wounding and criminal damage.

Being nearby, we responded and as we turned a corner into the street the pursuit was now on, the offender, a lad aged about 20, with a very athletic build and about 6ft, was running fast towards us, about fifty yards to the right of the vehicle I was driving. I shouted to my front passenger colleague that I was going across the footpath to head the lad off.

As I turned the vehicle towards the footpath, it was obvious that my colleague in the front passenger seat hadn't understood as she was about to bail out with her door open which could have seriously injured her if I'd continued the manoeuvre.

Next thing I recall I was off balance jumping out the vehicle and the lad about ten yards in front of me by now wasn't for stopping! I was still off balance as I was about to bring him down with an ankle tap. I brought him down, but it wasn't the ankle tap that did it as the offender shunted me with his forearm sending him and me crashing to the ground. I had been KO'd by the impact of the collision with his forearm, a plate glass shop window and then the footpath on the back of my head as I finally landed. I don't recall that, but I was informed by my colleagues who witnessed it, that was how it happened.

The Initial consequences:

I don't remember too much as I had been concussed, although I do remember the intense pain I was in especially from my neck, into my right shoulder and right arm. I was conveyed to hospital where I was treated for concussion, lacerations and bruising to the back of my head, severe neck pain, shoulder and arm pain, and numbness in my right hand. I was also in a severe neck spasm caused by the force of the assault, it was a severe whiplash injury, but thankfully, short of a broken neck. A neck x-ray showed no fractures but did show something I later discovered was called cervical lordosis, which triggered events in my spinal column and has impacted my life ever since.

I can't recall too much more of follow up treatment at that time other than outpatient and physio before eventual referral to a consultant orthopaedic surgeon. I wasn't off work too long, just a week or so I think, and although my neck pain seemed for a while to improve, my neck movement was quite restricted with pain and my right arm and shoulder were also restricted with pain and tingling continuing into my hand and fingers.

The Custody Office Injury:

Fast forward to 1992 and by now I was a sergeant working as a custody officer. One night shift in the custody office a detainee became violent as he was being processed before being put into a cell. When I went to assist the arresting officer, the prisoner punched me on my forehead and nose causing a cut and nosebleed and pain. That happened right in front of the duty solicitor who became a witness for us. I think that in itself is a rarity. I wasn't concerned about the nose much, but I knew my already damaged neck had been worsened.

It never improved after that, and I was eventually discharged as unfit for operational police duty and no office job or non-operational role was forthcoming.

The only time I was off sick from operational police work following both of my injury incidents, was when recuperating from the operations or the initial impacts of the injuries. But after New Year's Eve 1988, I was always working with so much pain and discomfort. I did my best to disguise this at work as I was about to be promoted to sergeant, which thankfully came about in early 1990. It was actually delayed though, because of a malicious complaint against me by a person I had apprehended for a crime for which he was later convicted. The Police Complaints' Procedure meant I could not be promoted until the outcome of the complaint, which only happened after his trial and conviction.

Specialist Treatment:

Once I got to see the consultant, which continued with appointments for five or so years after my police service discharge, I had surgery on my neck in 1998 which by then had deteriorated to the extent that the surgeon said to me in layman's terms, "Your x-rays show your neck is in an awful state." It was discovered with more tests and x-rays that I had a significant injury to my ulna nerve, which runs from my neck, through my right shoulder down my arm into my hand and fingers.

Between 1990 and 1993, I had two operations on the ulna nerve, 1, Ulna nerve surgical release, 2, Ulna nerve surgical transposition. Periods of neck and arm physio followed. I was back at work fully operational but continued with varying degrees of neck pain accompanied with violent headaches. I didn't want to go off sick as I had just been promoted.

Medical, Physical and Psychological Consequences:

Since the assault on New Year's Eve 1988, I have had three surgeries as a direct consequence on my right arm and my neck. Those injuries, or rather the impact of them, resulted in my discharge from the Police Service in February 1994. I received a certificate stating that my conduct had been 'exemplary'. That is the only recognition any police officer gets if they are discharged in similar circumstances.

I'm still under the care of specialists and I am likely to require further major surgery on my neck, as the damage now shown on scans is extremely bad and at levels in my neck where further surgery would come with no guarantee of improvement. I was told in 2017 by my then neurosurgeon it could even worsen things. So at that point I turned down three level spinal fusion surgery.

But as things have worsened for me since then, I'm now ready to see if there are new neurosurgical techniques that might help. I'm also now walking slowly with a stick as the damage to my neck, added to general arthritic changes through my back, significantly affect my balance as well as pain levels. Before my injury I enjoyed physical exercise, running, playing football and golf and leisure time out walking in the fells. Those activities to keep fit and healthy both physically and mentally came to an abrupt halt when I had been a fit and healthy relatively young man, and that was difficult to come to terms with, and even today it still is.

Life after the Police:

Unlike so many of my badly injured police colleagues, whose injuries not only prevented them continuing their police service, but also their ability to get back to any other employment, I was very fortunate. I was very low when I'd left, but with encouragement from my wife, and a welfare officer who was probably the best in the country (he'd been an operational police officer for most of his service and wanted the best for people in situations like mine), I was able to study to get academic qualifications which enabled me to have a supportive second career in the NHS, five years or so after my police career ended. In that job, I had a line manager who was fully aware of my physical difficulties.

My workplace was adapted to help me, but she and others valued my experience and skills developed in my police career, and the ones I'd added to in my own time. In effect it was the office / training job which wasn't on offer when I was discharged from the police. Ironically, part of my role in the NHS was working with emergency services including the police, delivering training to and with them on many occasions.

I'm fully retired now, having somehow managed to work almost forty years combined in serving the public. However, in terms of the impact and complexity of the police career ending injuries, they will remain with me for the rest of my life. Compared to those who lost their lives doing their job or are now paraplegics needing round the clock care for the consequences of their injuries sustained on operational duty, I am very fortunate.

Author's comment.

I could not help thinking whilst reading John's story of the basic simplicity of the 2 assaults that caused his promising career to be brought abruptly to an end.

These types of assaults happen every day to frontline officers throughout the UK. Those who suffer them, after treatment and a period of recovery, normally fully recover without any aftereffects.

Sadly, for poor John, he was unlucky not to be one of those.

John is a prime candidate for my medal proposal.

Kevin McNally

Kevin McNally

I was born in West London in 1952 and I left school in 1971 with O and A levels. I had a few jobs, telephone engineer, diesel fitter, cargo handler and as a territorial army soldier.

In 1976, I joined the Metropolitan Police and after completing training I was posted to the area that I'd grown up in.

I gained several different skills: firearms, public order, court presentation, street duties tutor, auto crimes and baton gunner.

I had just over twenty years in the same area, then with retirement looming up the job decided to implement a new policy of transferring officers to other divisions. I'd recently married, and my wife was due to have major surgery. I approached the Senior Management Team (SMT) and explained my situation. It didn't matter a jot, there was a box to be ticked. I was studying for a master's degree related to the job and I had just received my post graduate certificate. Tough, I was no longer the responsibility of my SMT. That was all down to my new one.

One harrowing incident which was the final straw and added to my mental stress was the case of a male who shot and killed a female and then took his own life in the same manner.

I felt totally abandoned, my knowledge and experience meant nothing, my welfare even less. I was very depressed and saw my GP who referred me to a consultant privately. He diagnosed me as suffering from PTSD. I approached the job which eventually referred me to Mr. Terry Wait, former consultant, who concurred with the original diagnosis and stated that my condition was acute.

How did the job react? They put me on a reduced wage whilst I was on sick leave. All this time I wasn't offered any help. It was all adversarial. They wanted me gone, but very cheaply.

I was offered an 'injury on duty' pension, but at a very low rate which I appealed and had it increased.

I finally retired in 1998. It had taken nearly two years to get to this stage. Not once was I offered any assistance from the job; I felt that I'd been cast aside.

I received my 'Long Service and Good Conduct Medal' and certificate in the post without so much as a covering letter. Some months later I was summoned to attend a medical examination in central London. The examining doctor really had no idea about PTSD and when I mentioned that I'd taken an overdose, he told me that I'd better get on with it then. Empathy, what empathy?

Author's comment.

This story indicates the lack of care or interest in the plight of good officers. There is no sympathy for those missing out on a medal and monumentally less where budgets are concerned!

Kevin is yet another example of those viewed as expendable and nothing more than collateral damage to be written off and gotten rid of and as cheaply as possible.

What a sad situation it is when an officer down on his luck whilst suffering from mental issues and at a time of vulnerability must find the strength from somewhere to fight for his rights or face being ripped-off financially, and without support from the fictitious police welfare system.

Andrea Brown

I am Andrea Brown and I served with Greater Manchester Police from 1980 to December 2010. The last 12 years of my service were on K Division Bolton, where I was the dedicated hospital liaison officer for the Royal Bolton Hospital.

On Monday 20th August 2007, I was on duty when I received a call from the hospital asking for police assistance. The doctor and the approved mental health practitioner (AMHP) were at an address and were going to section a male. This was a regular occurrence, and I thought there would be nothing different in responding to that call. Little did I know what was to follow and that on this occasion this call would change my life.

I did my normal police national computer person check and as a result of that I asked for the van to make its way to the address. I arrived at the address with the doctor and the AMHP. The van was on its way.

As we were waiting outside the address the male opened the door. There were a lot of children playing in the street and we had a quick discussion. We decided to go into the address with the male, rather than run the risk of him becoming aggressive in the public place.

Once in the address things took a drastic turn. I radioed for the van to attend as soon as possible. Without warning the male jumped up and ran to the kitchen and I requested urgent assistance. What followed remains with me to this day. The male grabbed at me, and I was trying to restrain him. What followed, I only know through the witness statements of the doctor and AMHP. As I was on the floor struggling with him, he hit me with a solid glass candle holder, but I don't remember anything else apart from shutting my eyes and thinking I'm going to die, be quick, I'm not going to see my mum or daughter again! He then dropped a glass table on top of me and rampantly scalped me by ripping my hair out from the roots.

Thankfully, I don't recall that or anything until the paramedics arrived.

Following the incident, the male was apparently too unwell to be charged with wounding assault and was sectioned. He never went to court.

The next 3 years were spent fighting the job to avoid being pensioned off. My pride wouldn't let that happen. I carried on and also spent the next few years being put before different psychologists and doctors and having to relive the horrors every time. I was diagnosed with PTSD and fibromyalgia as a result of the vicious attack and my near-death experience.

Here is what I suffered:

1.) The whole centre area of my scalp was torn, approx. 3 inches x 5 inches. Where there had been hair there were holes where the hair had been ripped out from the roots.

2.) The front of my forehead was glued rather than stitched to try to avoid scarring on my face.

3.) My arms and legs were swollen and bruised. Both my eyes were swollen and completely black.

4.) I had bruises on my body, arms and legs.

5.) It took 12 months for my hair to fully grow back and to this day that area is very sensitive.

6.) The pain was unbearable.

Approx 8 to 9 months later I was in the training office when a package arrived, you know how excited we all got when new uniform arrived and I thought that's what it was.

However, when I opened the parcel inside was my uniform from that dreaded day and still covered in blood. It was all taken from me in hospital for evidence and the worst part, all my blooded hair that had been ripped out was there too. This had been sent up from the police property store. As you can imagine, I went hysterical and had a full-blown panic attack... Good old job, eh!

I struggled on and finally retired after completing my 30 years and again the next few years still being sent to doctors and specialists.

Whilst in the job I did get support but once I left there was nothing. I was still waiting to go to court re criminal injuries and seeing doctors at the DWP who diagnosed me as 35% disabled. You have no support network and there is nowhere to go or turn to regarding your injuries.

Author's comment.

Poor Andrea was viciously attacked by a psychiatric patient and sustained horrendous injuries. I have seen the photographs of her bleeding and wounded scalp. I imagine the injury was similar to that inflicted upon victims by Native Americans in the past when scalps were taken as trophies of battle. The images are far too graphic to reproduce here. Suffice it to say that it appears that the whole top of her scalp was ripped away. The force needed to inflict such a harrowing injury must have been immense and the pain unbearable.

The returning of Andrea's blood-stained clothing that she'd worn that sad day and her ripped out hair exhibit was thoughtlessness beyond belief and from a member of the so-called 'police family'.

I note there was no mention of the two medical personnel getting injured or even involved in the defence of poor Andrea. She was only rescued when other officers arrived.

The determined Andrea, who had already received her 'LS & GC Medal' struggled on for another 3 years and retired normally after 30 years' loyal and dedicated service.

Although Andrea did receive the aforementioned 'medal' and completed her service, her story is rightly included here because her injuries both physical and mental were so severe that it highlights the dangers frequently faced daily by brave officers, in this case a female.

Stephen Court

Here is my personal story. I had served in my previous force for 17 years and 10 of those years were in frontline roles: response, neighbourhood policing and ports policing.

I attended a horrific death of a 15-year-old child at the hands of his mother. This hit me harder than I imagined, and I found myself looking to get away from frontline policing for a break.

My force was hit hard with the cuts. I moved into CID and did quite well after being promoted and I started taking on more responsibility.

Our force required all violent or unnatural deaths to be attended to by a detective sergeant which was fine when we had staff. Sadly, numbers reduced and coupled with COVID, I found it was just me attending these for my team. On many occasions the control room stacked these up for me to attend.

At the same time, I was accepted as a Hostage and Crisis Negotiator. COVID saw the numbers of deployments increase. I attended a really nasty negotiation where the subject did later kill himself. I had spent 6 hours talking to him like a friend.

I found myself at complete burn out. There were too many cases to list.

My force then posted me into Child Abuse investigation. Bang, suddenly without any awareness I suffered a horrific breakdown. PTSD was the cause.

I now suffer each night with vivid dreams taking me back to these scenes. I struggle to go about day-to-day life without breaking down. I am on what I suspect is lifelong medication and ended up leaving the job I had loved.

I am sure many out there have similar stories. What saddened me the most was the most undignified departure from my force. A quick exit interview and that was it, the end.

Author's comment.

Stephen's account shows how quickly one's services can be dispensed with and things just roll-on with someone else filling his vacant role, whilst he continues to suffer nightmares.

Kay and Garry Instrell

Kay Instrell *Garry Instrell*

I joined the Metropolitan Police in February 1974. It was one of the first intakes where women police worked alongside their male colleagues. I was also part of a duty roster that meant a female officer was available to cover the district. This didn't always work as we attended court the same day if an arrest was made on nights, or the next day if an arrest was made later in the day. It wasn't unusual for me to work from 10pm, attend court the next day at 10am and then work through the next day but still receive a call out to provide cover for the district.

I had a few 'assaults on police', bitten thumb etc. but nothing too bad. I married a PC in 1976 who worked in the neighbouring division, but we didn't work together and didn't want to.

I joined the British Transport Police in 1978. A different system with BTP meant that women had always worked alongside their male colleagues including policing football trains. BTP provided trousers (in the Met it wasn't the case unless you were on a specific section such as Mounted or Traffic). I was also given handcuffs unlike the Met. at that time.

Whilst travelling to night duty in our vehicle, my husband was driving, we witnessed a serious road traffic accident where the vehicle driven at speed missed the bend on the busy south circular road, hit a lamppost and rebounded on to a 17-year-old female pedestrian on the pavement. We approached the scene to assist but saw the male driver who had hit her decamp. We followed him in our vehicle and as he ran alongside the passenger side, I opened the door and knocked him to the ground.

I caught hold of him, but he managed to turn and hit me with his fist in the face. It was like I was seeing this in slow motion. I knew I couldn't let go as he was a fast runner but as his fist approached my face, I noticed he had a signet ring. This hit me on my mouth causing a 'Y' shaped cut to my face. My husband came to assist as he was still fighting, and we managed to get him to the floor. Luckily, I had my handcuffs. My husband was unaware that I was injured but saw the blood over the male and the ground and assumed he'd been injured in the crash.

We had stopped outside a bingo hall where people were leaving and when the public realised that he'd left a young girl severely injured they wanted to lynch him. I prevented this by lying over him. (I was glad of my trousers!) He was later to allege at court that he'd been 'beaten up by the police'!

I received 9 stitches in my face, the magistrate commented, "Did you have to show me this before my lunch?" on seeing police photographs of my face after being stitched. He got a three months' suspended sentence, not for injuring an innocent girl, driving under the influence in a stolen vehicle or even for hitting a police officer but for driving uninsured. (He'd appeared at court the day of the accident for having an offensive weapon.)

I did receive a criminal injury compensation payout, but I still have the physical scars on my face. My new nickname at work was Scarface, but that was the old-style police humour, and I would laugh after the stitches were removed.

I was also head butted when I was with a young male officer just out of training school. A male was being ejected from Euston station (it closed after the last train), but we strongly believed he was trying to proposition a young male and we needed to ensure he was safe. This was a common occurrence at Euston and a 'hunting ground' for paedophiles who looked out for vulnerable youngsters.

When he was removed, without warning he head butted me against a plate glass window. I did see stars but when I came around, I saw him beating my colleague. As he ran off, I chased him and managed to get him to the ground and call for assistance. I'm not sure if I lost consciousness but wanted to go to court with him in the morning so kept quiet. I had a few loosened teeth and a big headache. He pleaded not guilty and was given bail but absconded. I caught him three years later; you remember their faces when they've assaulted you and your colleague.

I had a few more 'assaults on police' but strangely not on the violent football trains where we were outnumbered 700 to 4 of us but you did need to keep your wits about you.

I was put on the first BTP Tactical Support Group. I had passed my sergeant's exam and was hoping to go up the ranks and this would help. My husband, after 9 years at Brixton was hoping to leave the Met. Our plan was for me to transfer hopefully as a sergeant to a BTP vacancy in Exeter. We had decided to buy a bookshop, a dream my husband had had for some years, he'd had enough of policing.

I was sent to shield training with the Met. The force initially refused to train women, but my male colleagues insisted I was an operational officer and not a radio operator like some of my colleagues. So, they gave me a trial day which I passed and once dressed in blue overalls, wearing a police helmet they'd forgotten I was a female.

I was sent to various public order incidents all over London and the suburbs. We were asked to assist the Met. They had wanted railway land searched for a murder weapon possibly discarded on an embankment. I climbed over the fence, the third of six officers but on landing felt my leg break, more than once.

We were going to sign the contract to buy a bookshop the following Monday so that my husband could resign. I believed I'd be sent to casualty, plastered and sent home later in the day. The doctor on seeing my x-rays said that my injury was, 'life-changing, and I'd never be able to walk the same way again'. I didn't believe him.

Two weeks in hospital for surgery, pins and plates inserted and 9 months of non-weight bearing, and I was still in severe pain. Further investigation revealed I'd got secondary arthritis and was offered an arthrodesis (fusion) or an ankle replacement.

I think I was still in disbelief and was sure I'd get back to normal. I was a trained athlete, a swimmer, I had represented British Police in their swim team, and I was a lifesaving and first aid champion.

I was sent to the medical officer. He bluntly told me that my ankle would never be good enough to resume normal duties and I'd have to be 'medically retired' as it wouldn't look right to have a limping police officer.

I received my medical discharge letter on the day WPC Yvonne Fletcher was murdered on duty. This helped me to realise that it could so easily have been me. I was lucky to get out alive and had a few close calls during football public order duties.

I finished on night duty and although on 'light duties' had managed to get a few good arrests using the security cameras in the control room. I thought they'd change their minds if they saw I was still capable.

I went on annual leave and the following weekend won a medal for swimming at the Cheshire Masters, an annual event for serving police officers and the first medallist for the BTP.

I received one welfare phone call in my first month and that was all. I receive a small pension and I have not worked professionally since my medical discharge. I have had numerous surgical procedures and even went for a 'below knee' amputation which the surgeon was happy to proceed with. He did want to try a procedure that would help reduce my pain and keep my leg but three operations later and I still have my full leg.

I was always a volunteer swimming teacher and as a result of my injury and subsequent disability I was asked to coach some disabled swimmers. Three ended up as Paralympic medallists. We started a competitive swim club for people with disabilities which is still going strong and has produced Paralympian world record holders and the youngest ever Paralympian medallist.

My husband never managed to get his bookshop but does volunteer at one for the local children's hospice.

He served 31 years in uniform but suffered his first heart attack at 45. Two subsequent heart attacks culminating in a triple bypass, and he retired to work another 9 years as a civilian with the Met.

I believe my injury contributed to Garry having health issues, his first of three heart attacks. Our lives changed in a second when I landed on the ground injured. We had little support from work, were in separate forces and there was no welfare from either of them. He continued in a job that he'd planned to leave as our income took such a dive and we still had to keep a roof over our heads.

Whilst looking after me when I was discharged from hospital, Garry tripped on the stairs fetching me a dressing gown and also broke a bone in his foot. We both attended fracture clinic together, but poor

Garry wasn't considered bad enough to warrant hospital transport, so I watched him struggle on crutches to get to hospital from my hospital transport. Our lovely postman offered to help us as we had no family around and there were 23 steps up to our front door.

We later moved to accommodation that was more disabled friendly. He served 31 years as a constable and nine years as a civilian. He now volunteers as a swim teacher, bookseller in a charity bookshop, poppy seller for the RBL and an occasional bowls player.

We had two children and when our youngest was a teen we took in two girls who would have been put into care due to family problems. It was called family and kinship fostering so we didn't receive any financial support, but Garry continued to work and support us all. One of the girls later married our son and we now have two grandchildren.

We would never encourage our children to join the police due to its dangers and lack of support to those who serve.

Author's comment.

A true man and wife 'police family' who gave a great part of their life to the Police Service.

Although her husband, Garry, did receive his well-deserved 'Long Service and Good Conduct Medal', Kay was deprived of the same only due to her injury. If she were to stand alongside her husband at any police event, with him proudly wearing his medal, she would be seen merely as his wife. Given her police service from 1974 to 1984 and health sacrifice that cannot be right and must be corrected.

Kay was obviously an extremely talented swimmer and her injury impacted on that. It is, however, admirable that she continues to pass on her knowledge both in swimming and disability to others by coaching to such a high standard.

The Police Service owes so much more to the Instrell 'police family' than they ever received!

John Burgess

John Burgess

My husband, John, was a serving police officer from 1972 to 2002. Seven years in the West Midlands force, followed by 23 years in Sussex.

In 2001, John was involved in a near fatal accident whilst on night duty when he was the passenger in a police traffic accident. He was knocked unconscious, swallowed his tongue with the force of the crash but fortunately one of the first officers on the scene was an ex-nurse and managed to clear the airways before he was cut out of the car and taken to the nearest accident and emergency hospital. He was revived twice at the scene and once again at the hospital.

The accident happened about 11.45pm and at approximately 1am I was awoken by that dreaded knock at the door. The officer made it obvious I needed to get to the hospital as soon as possible.

One of the first senior officers I encountered in the resuscitation room just said, "So I suppose you are going to sue us then?" No compassion whatsoever, bearing in mind at this stage I was unsure if my husband was going to live or not.

The colleague responsible for the accident was a Federation man and was given support from both the Federation and welfare department. My husband on the other hand was not treated the same, he received no help from either. I contacted the welfare department to express my disgust at the lack of help and support at the time.

My husband did go on to receive an injury on duty award and was pensioned out of the service. This should have been automatic but was not. He found out by pure chance and just within the time limit that he was entitled to one. When you are so badly injured and fighting for your life, money and suing someone is the last thing on your mind.

John today is 30% disabled, has memory loss, is in constant pain as a result of the injuries and can no longer pursue his main passion in life, golf.

He was one of the first on the scene of the Brighton bombing years before and carried an injured victim down several flights of stairs to safety. He had also been one of the first on the scene of the Birmingham pub bombings years earlier and never hesitated to go straight in to rescue the injured.

Every police officer injured on duty deserves so much better than the treatment they receive.

Author's comment.

There is little in this story to indicate any care or compassion and for an officer who had served for 30 years.

I note the reference to the different treatment of the 'Federation man' driver and John's. Perhaps a classic case of 'It's not what you know but who you know?'

Piers Lawrence

Piers Lawrence

I joined Northumbria Police in 1977, transferring to Durham in 1992.

I was a fully operational officer for my entire career, 3 years on traffic in Newcastle upon Tyne, and 11 years on traffic in Darlington. Like most officers, I was subject to my fair share of assaults, but you kept on going because it was part of your job, but you still had a respect for the greater public whom you had sworn to serve.

My 30 years' service was due to be completed on August 31st, 2007. However, I signed on for another year.

The weekend before I was due to finally retire, on Saturday 8th August 2008, I attended the scene of an injury road traffic accident (RTA) outside Darlington, to assist another colleague.

Having cleared up the scene, witnessed the air-ambulance depart, and helped-out the vehicle recovery contractor, I walked up the road to collect my signs and cones. Bear in mind that the site was a winding semi-rural derestricted road, so both approaches were extensively signed and coned, and the scene protected by two fully marked and illuminated patrol cars.

While I was walking up the edge of the road, a car approached. What happened exactly was described to me a day or two later, but it appears the driver didn't react to the advance warning signs, nor my high visibility presence in the road. The vehicle swerved and caught the nearside soft verge, flipped over and bounced towards me. Being unable to get out of the way, the car struck me and threw me into the air. I landed in a motionless heap on the road. The car landed upside down nearby.

Had it not been for my colleague's presence, I probably wouldn't have survived the large and heavily bleeding head wound which was just one of several injuries I sustained, including a broken right fibula, dislocated left shoulder and associated facial injuries.

I was airlifted to James Cook University Hospital at Middlesbrough where I spent two weeks and had surgery to repair some fracturing around the dislocated shoulder.

Six to eight months of subsequent physiotherapy and recovery saw me back up and about again, but it took longer for me to heal mentally.

I must point out that the support given by my immediate colleagues was fantastic. My direct supervisors were great, and in particular the shift inspector who went above and beyond in providing support post incident.

The twist in this tale is that I received no injury on duty award. I was due to retire in a few days' time, and I had already submitted a report to request a finishing date.

The Chief Constable declined to rescind the report, which effectively meant that I was unable to subsequently claim for loss of earnings etc.

The insurance claim for the collision took three years to finalise, so what I was eventually awarded was only on a sliding injury scale. In the greater scheme of things, I'm lucky to still be here to relate the story, many others have suffered far worse than I. The point is that the organisation didn't push itself to provide support, it took other individuals to put themselves out to try and bring about a more successful resolution.

Author's comment.

There is no doubt whatsoever in my mind that Piers was robbed of his deserved 'injury on duty award'. It simply does not make any logical sense to accept that because he had already tendered his resignation that he was no longer eligible to receive it. He was on police duty, and he was injured and it's as simple as that. It is my opinion that he was seriously misinformed and indeed misled by those who told him otherwise.

I accept the IOD award sum may not have been a huge amount because of him having served the full-term 30 years' service but nevertheless he was eligible irrespective of any pending submitted 'resignation'.

Piers says himself that the support he received came from individuals rather than the Police Service.

I find it really sad that Piers had already completed his 30-year term but had decided to sign up for another year and only had about 3 weeks of that to complete, when he was injured. Hindsight is a great thing but if only he'd retired at his right time, eh?

Lee Neale

Lee Neale

In the spring of 2003, I embarked on a journey with the Avon & Somerset Constabulary, fuelled by a passion for making a difference. My early days on response teams were a blend of adrenaline and purpose, setting the stage for a dream I held close to join the firearms unit.

In 2007, that dream took shape, but not without its trials. The culture within the unit was a barrier I hadn't anticipated, and I found myself returning to response policing, carrying with me lessons in resilience and the unshakable spirit of a protector.

2009 marked a new chapter as I joined the Support Group. It was here that I encountered the stark realities of policing, from body recovery operations with deeply distressing scenes to the massive disorder of events that no one would officially label a riot. It was during these intense moments that I sustained not just a physical injury but also deep mental scars, a silent battle that began to take its toll.

Throughout my career, I had never received formal training in body recovery, in managing the aftermath of such harrowing experiences, nor was any mental health support offered.

The command decisions of the time, meant to control chaos, often left a lingering sense of unrest in my mind. Despite this, I continued with unwavering dedication, eventually transitioning to the Chemical, Biological, Radiological, and Nuclear (CBRN) unit. My role expanded beyond the frontline to logistical support, often at murder scenes and tragic road accidents. Providing necessary but grim resources like lighting towers and body bags, I was a silent witness to countless traumatic events. Yet, in a role not traditionally recognized for its emotional toll, the psychological support I so needed was absent.

Through these experiences, I've come to understand the immense weight of service and the often-unseen impact it has on those who serve. While my physical injuries have healed, the mental wounds are a testament to the sacrifices made in the line of duty. My journey has been one of courage, resilience, and an unwavering commitment to serve, even in the face of personal adversity.

As the years passed, the weight of my experiences began to manifest in ways I hadn't anticipated. I became increasingly anxious, a constant undercurrent in my daily life. Depression cast a shadow over my once vibrant spirit, and anger became an all-too-frequent companion. Simple moments with my family were overshadowed by a relentless hyper-vigilance. Every approaching car seemed like a potential threat, every stranger a possible perpetrator of unimaginable acts. These were the silent, insidious symptoms of PTSD, a battle I was fighting alone, unaware of its name.

In the world I served, the culture was unforgiving. "If you can't take it, you shouldn't have joined," they'd say. This mantra echoed in the halls, silencing cries for help, including my own. A lack of support and understanding or even an acknowledgement of the mental toll of what our duties entailed, were scarce. I tried to bury these feelings, to lock them away, but they only grew stronger and more demanding.

July 2019 marked a turning point: I experienced what can only be described as a nervous breakdown. I was forced to step away from my duties, hoping for a respite, a chance to heal. But the cycle repeated – a brief return to work followed by another period of sickness. This pattern continued until December 2022, when I was retired on an ill-health pension.

Author's comment.

Lee had his share of upsetting incidents to deal with and it unfortunately took a great toll on his psychological welfare, and this cut short his service.

He sadly says support was absent, but he too also left the service without a medal to show his police connection or health sacrifice.

Kimberley Christie-Sturges

PC Kimberley Christie-Sturges

What do you want to do when you grow up? I can remember being asked. Be a police officer or air stewardess was always my reply. I always knew that a career in the police offered more security, a career that would expand 30 years.

So, at the age of 18, I started looking and saw an advert for police specials. I knew nothing about them at all, so I enquired as Greater Manchester were doing a recruiting campaign. I came from a town called Stockport which is South Manchester and thought I could do this. I was young, ambitious and the fact you didn't get paid for the job, only expenses, didn't matter. It would give me a taster to see if I liked it and boy did I. I loved it, I tried to fit in as many shifts as I could between working in a bakery. I wanted to get as much experience as possible, and I loved the camaraderie. I felt like I belonged, I was valued, and I had a place.

I was a special for four years but felt I wanted more. Greater Manchester Police were not recruiting but the Metropolitan Police in London were. So, I applied and after attending interviews in London and fitness tests I was accepted.

I remember the day so well, packing up my car and heading for the capital on the 17th of March 1985. I felt so guilty as it was Mother's Day. I hadn't really thought what the effects of moving would be on my family, I guess I was caught up in the whirl of it all. They struggled for a long time after I left.

After five months of training, I was sent to Clapham. Where on earth is Clapham, I thought? I soon discovered it was south of the River Thames and it covered the borough of Lambeth. I lived in a police section house opposite Clapham Common which comprised of rooms and shared facilities. I soon settled in making new friends, learning all the skills of being a police officer in London which was very different than what I had been used to. This was full on, very diverse and extremely rewarding. My mum kept asking, "When are you moving back?" I always replied, "I'm not, this is my life now."

Then on the 25th of August 1986, I was on early turn which started at 7am and would normally finish at 3pm. A call came into the station at 8am of reports of a youth trying to break into cars. I was the passenger in the police area car. "We will take it," was my reply and off we went. As we arrived, I could see a youth further up the road on the pavement so I asked my colleague to drop me, and I would walk up as I couldn't properly see what he was doing.

As I got closer, I could see that a car had been broken into by the glass on the floor and then saw the youth trying to break into another one further up the road. He saw me and started to run. I looked around for our car and I couldn't see it, so there was no option but to run after him. I shouted over the radio that I was chasing, where I was and a description of the guy.

He ran across Clapham High Street with me running behind him. Luckily, there was no traffic coming. Now I was never the fastest runner in the world, I had always relied on my northern charm but not today. We ran down a one-way street and I kept looking for the car, where was it? I managed to catch up with the youth and shouted proudly, "I'm arresting you for criminal damage," to which he said, "No you are not!"

Suddenly, I felt my head hit a low wall as I was pushed to the ground. My hands went from holding his jacket to holding his trouser bottoms. I kept thinking you are not getting away from me even though my head hurt so much. He kept kicking and kicking me and all that I can ever remember was white trainers. To this day I can't look at white trainers without being transported back to that day. To be honest after the first few kicks I didn't feel anything except the overwhelming feeling of don't let go of him. I'm guessing that must have been the adrenaline in my body.

When backup eventually came, apparently, they had to prise my fingers off his trousers as I had gripped so hard. I will never know why it took my colleague driving the car with me that day so long to get there or where he had been. He didn't stay long at my station after that and was due to retire soon after.

Apparently, when I was taken to the hospital, I had the perfect imprint of finger marks around my neck which were consistent to being strangled, yet I had no recollection of him ever touching my neck. I had long hair which I had put into a tight bun. The doctor said that he believed that it saved my skull on that day. It must have been that that had hit the wall first.

I had bruising to my back, which was so painful, my neck and he had chipped one of my front teeth. But thankfully nothing was broken.

My sister drove down and took me back home to recover and they tried their best to keep me there and to not return to London. A couple of weeks later, I felt I needed to get back to work and continue with the job I loved.

The 6 foot, 16-year-old lad that I had arrested received 3 months in a young offenders' institute. The judge was appalled at what he had done to me and said he had no option but to give a custodial sentence. I have never ever felt bitter towards the youth even though he did change my life and because of him my career was cut short. I guess it was the fight or flee in him on that day because he had committed a crime and unfortunately, I got in his way, even if it was just me doing my duty.

A year later I accepted a post in the Youth and Community section of the police which was dealing with schools and young offenders. In hindsight this wasn't the best move.

I thought I was fine, and everything had mended. How wrong was I? My back and neck still hurt but working on the unit helped. I began to notice the pain I was in when it was cold and how I couldn't open my jaw like I used to. I just put up with it thinking it's going to get better, but it didn't. I saw my doctor who sent me to see a specialist at St Thomas's Hospital.

After a year or so of treatment I had an operation on my jaw. I hadn't even thought about where the cut was going to be to get into the jaw. Even when the nurse put a cap on my head and the doctor said we will shave it later the penny didn't drop. I woke up to find stitches along my ear and into the hairline. When I had been kicked the jaw had basically compressed and had mended that way. The operation wasn't a success, but it was worth the try.

The thing that I never expected was my feelings when I saw my face. This was now five years after the assault but to me it was the same day. The emotions that went through my head were crazy I now know this was the start of PTSD. I had always been a bubbly, happy person with great tenacity which had been the theme on my yearly police reports. I wasn't that person anymore. Yet the thoughts or possibilities of being assaulted again filled me with fear. That day affected me not only physically but mentally as well.

In 1993, I was medically retired due to being injured on duty. The decision was made at a time when unless you could do all the roles of a police officer you were no longer employable. This policy has now thankfully changed and had it come in earlier, I would have completed my 30 years' service.

I still suffer with the pain in my lower back and in my neck from the incident on a daily basis. I know my jaw will never be right and I guess you learn to accept the pain. I struggle to stand for any length of time. When the kids were younger, I could never put them on my shoulders or give them piggy backs. My injuries have stopped me from doing a lot of things that others take for granted and continues to have an impact on my life.

In 2005, I proudly watched with our two daughters when my husband got his 'Long Service and Good Conduct Medal' at Hendon, which he received after 22 years. Sadly, something I was never to get. Yet had I not been injured and carry the scars and injuries to this day, I would have not only completed my 22 years but also undoubtedly would have gone on to complete 30 years with a full pension, instead of a very small one.

No medal exists for people like me, nothing. No recognition is given to the sacrifice we make, and I know my injuries are nothing to what others have suffered. Some have gone on to make the ultimate sacrifice, their lives, yet they also receive no recognition. This can't be right, can it?

Sadly, if a medal is ever approved my youngest daughter will never see me be awarded it, as she was killed in a road traffic accident in 2012, aged just 19 years old and then followed by my son-in-law in 2014, again a road traffic accident.

When you become a police officer you are led to believe that you become part of a family. Sadly, when you hand your warrant card over there is no support, you are on your own, it's not like the military where you can get support from agencies like the Royal British Legion. You are totally on your own.

All I was doing that day was just my job, doing my duty. Something that I had always wanted to do and one that I was really good at, but I was cut short in my prime by just doing my damn job!

Author's comment.

Kimberley tells her story so genuinely and eloquently that I cannot help being deeply touched and saddened. If that was not enough, I shed a tear on hearing her later family losses.

Her story has so many similarities to that of Angie McLoughlin, which began this section, that it is uncanny. I invite you to compare the two to see what you think BUT the main observation you should take is the sheer courage and determination of them both.

These two brave lasses, along with everyone else MUST receive their deserved medal recognition, no matter how late in the day! I'm going to continue to fight like hell to bring that about!

Roy Saunders

Roy Saunders

I joined the Metropolitan Police on 24th May 1982, and I was initially posted to Barnet police station.

I enjoyed a varied career after my initial posting. I spent time on the Territorial Support Group, Force Intelligence Bureau, Area Major Investigation and ahead of promotion to sergeant a brief spell on the Crime Squad and CID.

In November 1999 I had been reviewing CCTV footage at the Video Forensic Lab in Denmark Hill, when on the way back to the office I was involved in an accident riding my own motorbike but authorised to use it on duty. While stationary at the Elephant & Castle roundabout I was struck from behind by a very slow-moving car.

Initially I was able to keep my balance by 'paddling' ahead of the still pushing car, ultimately having to jump clear of an oncoming bus from my right in the middle of the roundabout. I hit the ground on the tip of my left shoulder with the bike falling onto my right knee. I remember being 'blue lighted' to the nearby St. Thomas's Hospital, where after some initial x-rays and examination I was released home for the night.

After an initial 14-day period of sickness absence I returned to work with a limp and a very painful left shoulder. Both joints had some swelling and mobility issues from the outset. There then followed a period of 18 months' physiotherapy, consultations, and various treatments to ascertain the exact nature of the injuries I had suffered. I continued to be at work with very little absence other than for planned medical appointments.

Roll on to my first surgery, post the accident, March 2001. I awoke from surgery to repair part of the damage to my shoulder with the immortal words of the surgeon, "Well, Mr. Saunders, I suggest you consider alternative employment. Your shoulder injury will mean the end of your career." I never went back to work for the Met. Police after that date.

I was off for 6 months on full pay, 6 months on half pay and 6 months with no pay. I had recently been posted to a new station, so I was not well known or established there. I felt that there was no local support offered to me at all. In the 18 months I was off I initiated all of the contact with the line management. I appealed the decision to move to no pay, but this was dismissed on the grounds that I was not engaged in the act of defence of violence at the time. It was simply a car accident.

I asked to be ill-health retired but this was refused on the grounds that it would cost too much for the pension payment and there were reviews of awards at the time. While I did have over 20 years' service I had only paid into the pension fund for the initial 7 years of my service as I did not see myself being with the Met. Police for as long as I was. Hence my own pensionable service was very low and of very little financial consequence. It was not until I requested a further medical appointment and review of pension forecast that I was eventually ill-health retired because of an injury on duty. This took from March 2001 until October 2002, by which time I had 20 years and 5 months' service.

My final visit to a Metropolitan police station was to a retirement interview with the Holborn Chief Superintendent a person whom I had never met prior to the interview. There were very few words other than the ringing of, "Don't forget to leave your locker key. They're like gold dust around here."

And that was that. OR was it...?

When the service time for the 'Long Service and Good Conduct Medal' was reduced from 22 to 20 years, I wrote to the Met. Police asking for a review of my circumstances and consideration being given to me

being awarded a 20-year LS & GC medal. I got a short reply stating that there must be a cut-off date and I was outside of it. Sorry. So that really was that.

I really enjoyed my time as a police officer, and I would honestly say that I'd do it all again. Just leave out the very bitter ending, the four and half years of waiting for an uninsured claim to go through the Motor Insurer's Bureau and the legacy now of two replacement knees and one replaced shoulder.

Author's comment.

Roy was on duty at the time of the accident and although he was using his own motor-cycle that is normal practice and any officer authorised to do so receives a mileage allowance.

He did not receive a 'Long Service and Good Conduct Medal' because during his time the eligibility period was 22 years. That was reduced to 20 years in 2010 but he along with many others was robbed again of it because the reduction was not made retrospectively.

Financially, more could be done for genuine cases when an injury on duty causes absence from work than that quoted i.e. '6 months full pay, 6 months half pay and 6 months no pay'. Money concerns and how to support oneself and a family will negatively impact on recovery and not aid it.

Martin Webster

I joined Lancashire Constabulary in 1995 (22 yrs. old) initially as a special constable (SC). It soon became apparent that I had found something I was good at, and my sole focus was to become a substantive officer in Lancashire. Thankfully, I was successful in becoming a police constable, continuing to work at Blackpool where I had been as a SC.

On 15th July 2000 whilst arresting a suspect my thumb was torn back by the suspect resulting in me being put in plaster for 6 weeks by the local A&E. It soon became apparent that the injury had not healed, and my thumb was dislocated permanently, and the hand surgeon said there was nothing he could do.

Thankfully, I had a very experienced sergeant who was also the local Federation representative and he made sure it was all documented and reported correctly and little did I know the importance of this in years to come.

I started soon after to study for my sergeant's exams and was promoted to shift sergeant and then neighbourhood sergeant. Unfortunately, the arthritis in my hand over the years got worse and the pain increased. I was unable to do the basic officer safety training and in 2010 the decision to start the ill-health process commenced. This is a very stressful and lengthy process which the Federation supported me through. However, it then became a waiting game, once the medical people had made their decisions and observations. I was told that the file was waiting for the 'Chief' to sign it off.

I was still leading my team of community officers (albeit office based) up to the day I got 'the call'. It was the 29th of December 2011, a lady called and said, "The Chief has signed your paperwork, as of midnight tonight you are no longer a police officer."

That was it. I finished my shift and drove home. It was surreal and definitely hadn't sunk in. I was quite shocked that 16 years of exemplary service could end so abruptly. I was only a month away from receiving the Queen's next Jubilee medal (Diamond Jubilee Medal) as you had to be in service on 6th February 2012. This seemed unfair as retired officers don't get considered.

During my career I received a number of commendations, for leadership and for my actions in a case involving the murder of a child and it all ended with a phone call. I was also within 4 years of receiving my 'Long Service and Good Conduct Medal' for which again retired officers are not considered. What I did get was a certificate in the post (no frame).

One thing I will say is that the Chief Superintendent from my division did call me and he too was shocked at the way I had been dealt with and the timing of 'the call'. He invited me in in the New Year to see him and the superintendent and they were very supportive. Having to go to the enquiry desk, get a visitor's pass and then be escorted to their office after working there for 16 years though is not a nice feeling.

The next 18 months or so were quite challenging for my mental health. I was very lost, I described it as having lost my identity, I was very low in mood, put on anti-depressants and waited a year for NHS counselling. I think these are some of the things that retired officers have to deal with that perhaps isn't or wasn't considered. To the organisation I guess it was just a process and the end of that process was to receive a phone call saying the Chief had signed you off.

Over the years my mental health has suffered, and I have had several surgeries on my thumb and the pain has never gone. Yes, I have my police pension, but money isn't everything. I think officers that are retired and particularly those who are retired through ill-health are not offered the support they deserve. If your service is ended through no fault of your own why can you not be considered for inclusion in the award of medals and for ongoing support?

Author's comment.

Martin's story highlights the simplistic way a career-ending injury can be caused.

I know from my own nephew's (not police) dominant hand thumb injury (and severe PTSD) how debilitating it can be. For example, buttons cannot be fastened but there are many other tasks that can no longer be performed.

I was stunned to read that Martin received an unexpected phone call dispensing with his services at midnight that day. There must be more compassion shown to an injured and loyal officer than that inappropriate way.

John Goodall

John Goodall

I joined the Halifax Borough Police in 1962 and served until 1987 but by that time the force was then part of the West Midlands Police. In 1987 I was medically discharged as the result of an injury sustained on duty.

In 1968 I became a dog handler and my injury occurred in 1977, when I was called upon to attend the scene of a burglary on the NW side of Birmingham a 20 + mile drive from where I happened to be at the time of the call.

By the time I reached the location I was left on my own to carry out a widened search for the suspect or suspects, who had made off on foot. Other officers had attended, done an initial search of the area but had stood down and resumed their other duties. This was a normal occurrence.

My dog picked up a track and about an hour after my call I found a male suspect on a building site some distance from the attacked premises.

The next part I still have nightmares about and all I will say is that there was a serious confrontation which resulted in both my dog and me being injured and the suspect evading capture. I am not willing to re-live the events and that is all the detail I wish to give of that part.

The injury to my dog was superficial but mine transpired to be extremely serious and life-changing.

After the event, I found that I had lost the use of my right side and because of the unreliable radios of the time, I could not summon assistance. I had no choice but to struggle back to Coventry driving as best as I could, and I went straight to the hospital.

I required spinal surgery but against all odds it was successful and with a little more difficulty I was able to continue my service and still as a dog handler. However, I needed numerous further operations.

In 1985, my specialist said that 'enough was enough' and that it would be prudent to give up the dog-handling job I loved and move to a less physical department. This I did and became a scene of crimes officer.

In 1987 my injury deteriorated, and it was decided that I would be medically discharged from the service. It was accepted that my injury had occurred on duty back in 1977 and that was the grounds for my discharge, but strangely I have never received a penny extra from any 'injury on duty award'.

At first, I received sympathy and indeed support from individual colleagues but not from the Police Service, Welfare or the Federation. Once I left, I felt that I'd been cast aside and onto the scrapheap of humanity.

It took 20 years for me to receive a nominal amount from the Criminal Injuries Compensation Board. This in fact allowed my wife and I to finally have a holiday, that was in 1999 and had we known just how ill I really was we would have never ventured on a foreign holiday.

In February 2000, due to all the stress caused by my invalidity and the financial situation we found ourselves in, as I could not work, I had serious heart problems. I had a heart attack, and this led to me 'dying' before arriving in the operating theatre of Southampton Hospital. The surgeons did a remarkable job, and I am still around to relate this story.

Even now, I am still trying to sort out why I have never received any money from having my injury accepted as an 'injury on duty award' and solicitors are trying to resolve it.

For many years I have existed on strong painkillers, including morphine.

Since retiring in 1987, I have been assessed by the Department of Work and Pensions as being 75% disabled, but I have never been assessed by the Police Service in any way, shape or form.

In 1989 I moved to Dorset, and I relied on both crutches and a wheelchair to assist mobility.

In 1995, I received a spinal implant which did give some relief, with me now on my third implant of this. However, I did and still do need the crutches to mobilise along with my NHS wheelchair.

Of course after my leaving the police my finances took a huge dip and I've not been able to be employed since.

I have received little if any support from the Police Service, but I have from a charity. It was called The Police Dependents' Trust. This is now called Police Care UK. Without their help I do not know what I would have done. They bought me over the years, two cars, a motorised and manual wheelchair and paid for home adaptations. They have been wonderful, but they are a charity and not the Police Service.

In 1993, I had the occasion to contact a welfare officer from Dorset Police, who contacted the West Midlands Police on my behalf. I was shocked when he later informed me that WMP had said that collar number 1479 had never been issued and they had no record of a John Goodall ever having served.

That sums it all up!

Author's comment.

Although John received his 'Long Service and Good Conduct Medal' I am still including his story in this section because he was injured on duty but has had to approach a police charity for financial assistance. This in itself indicates the failures in the system and the plight of an injured officer.

I find it most odd that John says his injury was accepted as being sustained on duty, but he receives no financial remuneration from that.

It is also sad that he is reduced to relying on assistance from a charity rather than from the Government or Police Service. It is clear that John needs the charity help otherwise he would not have been granted it because obviously his financial situation will have been thoroughly 'means tested'. Quite rightly charities ensure only the needy receive awards.

Clive Norman

Clive Norman

I joined the Metropolitan Police in 1990 and was engaged on uniform response.

In 1996 I attended an incident and was shot with a machine-gun by armed raiders as I attempted to stop their getaway, but I vowed to return to frontline duty.

I recovered well at St Thomas's Hospital in central London from a gunshot wound to my left calf. I admitted I felt lucky to be alive, but I added, "I'll be back as soon as I can. I'd like to think it won't affect me, but who knows?"

I had pursued the three armed robbers after they threatened a security guard with a gun and stole cash from a Security Express van outside the Nat West bank in Stockwell, south London. As I tried to stop one of the raiders jumping into the getaway car, a gun was pointed first at my head, then at my chest, and finally fired into my leg.

As the search for the robbers continued, I described the incident for the first time from my hospital bed. I said, "The whole thing just happened so quickly, my mind almost went blank, and I went into auto-mode. As far as I can remember I was standing in front of this gunman with some sort of weapon, and it was fired and one of the bullets hit my leg. Some would say I was brave, and some would say I was foolish. I don't know what made me do something like that.

"I don't know if I would react like that again but the only thing I regret is getting shot."

My being shot back then was only the second time a policeman in Britain had been hit by automatic gunfire and the latest in a long line of violent attacks on unarmed policemen and women.

I called for officers to be routinely given protective clothing but stopped short of calling for the police to be armed. However, I did express my anger at the amount of weapons falling into the wrong hands on the streets.

At that point in time, I had been with the Metropolitan Police for six years, and at the time I gave a warning about the gang which shot me, "They are obviously very dangerous men who didn't think twice about firing at a police officer and we can't have people like this on the streets."

After only 2 months, I somewhat amazingly did return to active policing.

In 2002, whilst chasing suspects over garden walls I fell 8 feet and injured my lower back and was hospitalised initially. I was released after three days but I continued suffering from back pain.

In 2006, I began to show signs of PTSD, in addition to the two injuries I'd suffered. In 1993 my close friend and colleague, Police Constable Patrick Dunne was shot and murdered by a drugs dealer. In 1995 a stabbing victim died in my arms whilst I tended him.

In 2009, the pain from both my leg and back injuries worsened and deprived me of sleep and it was decided to medically discharge me from the Police Service.

I would describe the transition as not being straightforward and because of my physical and mental state at the time, I did not fully comprehend what was happening. I had no visits or support from the Federation or Welfare and there was no one on hand to fully explain the procedure.

I received no medal recognition. I did receive my 'Certificate of Service' through the post. It was unframed, bent and crumpled. I felt that this was the 'final slap in the face'.

Author's comment.

This brave former officer deserves medal recognition in relation to his valuable contribution to the Police Service and his continued health sacrifice. He is a prime candidate for my campaign.

Kris Aves

Kris Aves

On Wednesday 22 March 2017, 52-year old British-born Khalid Masood drove a hired vehicle across Westminster Bridge in the direction of the Palace of Westminster. He mounted the pavement twice colliding with pedestrians and then a third time crashing into the east perimeter gates of the Palace of Westminster.

Masood then exited the car and ran into the vehicle entrance gateway of the Palace of Westminster, Carriage Gates, where he attacked and fatally injured PC Keith Palmer using a knife.

Masood was shot at the scene by armed police protection officers who were in Parliament at the time of the attack. The whole incident lasted approximately 82 seconds. The attack resulted in 50 people being injured and 6 fatalities.

I was a Metropolitan police officer, then aged 36, and I was hit by the terrorist on Westminster Bridge in 2017. I was leaving an award ceremony at New Scotland Yard and heading to Lambeth when hit. I sustained a spinal cord injury, and I am paralysed from the waist downward, and I am confined to a wheelchair for life. I was subsequently medically discharged from the Police Service.

I came out of an induced coma eight days after I was first injured, and I faced up to the reality of never walking again. I don't remember one minute of the attack. The last thing I recall is leaving New Scotland Yard having picked up a police award for my role in the BREXIT protests in and around Westminster earlier in the year. I was walking across the bridge to celebrate with a few beers and a burger with my colleagues when the attack occurred.

After the injury, any initial idea of me continuing my golfing hobby seemed impossible, but six years later I teed off. I now take part in the seating category thanks to a mobility device called a ParaGolfer that lifts me into an upright position. Thanks to ParaGolfer I was able to take my first shot as a disabled golfer, and it brought tears to my eyes.

I was in a dark place when I was told about my injuries and that it was a terrorist attack. I was paralysed from the chest down but following months of intensive treatment at Stoke Mandeville I set myself three main goals. To be the best dad I could be to my two children, to continue following my beloved Tottenham Hotspur FC and to play golf again. I achieved them all. My determination to return to the sport I love has made a dream come true by playing in the G4D Open.

However, I still face daily battles with severe spasms and nerve pains and the difficulty of golf shots without being able to turn my legs or hips.

Whilst I was in hospital, the TV programme DIY SOS, along with 300 people from my local community, transformed my home, making it fully wheelchair accessible.

I was offered office roles within the police after hospital but due to my injury, the medication I was on which caused tiredness and a lack of concentration, I decided, along with the medical officer, that ill-health retirement was the best option.

The ill-health retirement procedure took quite a long time due to the COVID pandemic, but I was supported and on full pay throughout.

Author's comment.

Kris was born in 1981 and joined the Metropolitan Police in October 2008, when he was 27 years old. He was only 36 years of age when he was injured. He was officially on duty.

Kris was supported financially by remaining on full pay throughout the pandemic and up until his retirement. I believe this was only due to his injury being a nationwide story and is not normally the case as will have been noted when reading the previous story contributions.

I'm hearing that Kris was supported by local people in his town and a TV show but not much of any Police Service support. I know he was visited by the Met. Commissioner whilst recovering in hospital but that too is not the norm and was much more than other injured officers receive. Their stories were not high profile but nonetheless are just as worthy. As I said early on in the book, as far as I'm concerned, it's not how the injury occurs that matters it's the severity.

His catastrophic injury not only severely impacted on him but on his partner and their two young children. Their lives too changed forever.

The only thing Kris has to show any police connection is a paper 'Certificate of Service' and that cannot be pinned to his chest on police occasions when he is likely to be viewed as a mere outsider.

Kris is a worthy candidate to receive a medal arising out of my proposal and I'm sure his family would appreciate the recognition of his police service and how tragically it was cut short.

Surely, we must all owe this young family a debt of appreciation for Kris's public service and their sacrifice?

Graham Savage

Graham Savage

I joined the Warwickshire Constabulary from 1975 and served there until 2005 and I retired in the rank of sergeant.

I have signed up to support Tom Curry's campaign to secure recognition for police officers medically retired following injuries sustained on duty. I am disappointed by the apparent lack of support from within the present Police Service.

I was the full-time Police Federation Secretary for Warwickshire Police between 1987 - 2005 and the Regional Secretary for Warwickshire, West Mercia, West Midlands & Staffordshire from 2001 - 2005.

The role of a Police Federation Secretary was essentially to monitor and negotiate conditions of service for their electorate. To this end the role also encompassed ensuring wherever possible injury on duty pensions were awarded where appropriate and in representing such pensioners who were necessarily required to appeal efforts to nullify or reduce such pensions.

In most instances in my experience IOD awards were considered favourably, certainly by Warwickshire but I did have cause to represent (successfully) a review of one of my pensioners.

Policing is not simply a 9 to 5 job; it is a vocation and a worthy one. Officers are routinely required (not asked) to put their lives and personal safety on the line to protect the public at large. Even with the modern advent of stab resistant vests, CS sprays and tasers, many officers do get injured or worse. Their intervention is expected and welcomed. Serious injury is not, but that is unfortunately an inevitable outcome sometimes.

An IOD pension award does not in itself recognise or reward the sacrifice police officers make in the line of duty. It is not a legacy that can be shown to their children or grandchildren, unlike the physical or emotional scarring, which is.

I believe and always have believed that a formal recognition in the form of a dedicated medal is warranted.

Author's comment.

I am truly grateful to 'old school' Federation man, Graham for his contribution. I note his disappointment in the reluctance of his successors to support the campaign.

CHAPTER 4

THE CAMPAIGN BEGINS

After reading all of these horrendously sad cases no one can possibly believe that the sacrifices should continue without those officers being recognised with a mere medal and it is a must for my much-needed campaign to continue to seek that.

It was way back in 2010, when the criterion for the 'Long Service and Good Conduct Medal' was reduced to 20 years but not made retrospective, that I first thought of the injustice of it all and I decided to mount my first campaign to correct it.

However, with no social media the broadcasting of it was difficult. I got no offer of support from the Police Federation or National Association of Retired Police Officers when I approached them. I do not like to refer to it as having failed but I much prefer to say it did not succeed, on that occasion.

Fast forward to 2023, when I first became aware of the campaign started by the father of murdered PC Nicola Hughes, who I previously referenced. This poor man, Bryn Hughes, continues to grieve over the loss of his child and in such terrible circumstances but without any posthumous medal recognition. How disgraceful that he had to be the one to begin the campaign to correct this national shame. The same applies to me as regards those injured.

I contacted Bryn and offered my support and since then we have spoken on the phone quite often. He is a fine and decent man.

One must wonder how many, Prime Ministers, Home Secretaries, MPs, Met. Police Commissioners, Chief Constables, Senior Police Officers, National Association of Retired Police Officers and Police Federation representatives there have been in the last 200 years, and why they did not correct this scandal before now, eh?

I believe the answer is that no one except those affected really care enough to do something and everyone who might be aware of the problem merely thinks that someone else will deal with it.

I noticed that there was no mention of the 'injured' in the latest posthumous award discussions and I spotted what I believed to be a flaw in the proposal, my attention being drawn to it by the previously mentioned case in Bradford in 2005. To re-cap, PCs Sharon Beshenivsky and Teresa Milburn were shot. Sharon was sadly killed but Teresa was saved.

Therein lies the flaw in the pending posthumous award because when it is approved, the 'fallen' will be recipients. If it is made retrospectively then those I mentioned, will receive it too. However, what about poor Teresa? She will be overlooked again. Imagine how you would feel in her situation.

This cannot be allowed to happen and with that I decided it was time to re-start my shelved campaign for the injured and that is exactly what I did.

In August 2023, I began my willing but arduous challenge. I realised that broadcasting the campaign this time would be easier due to social media. I also believed that only unity would bring about change.

I started saying the following:

'Nobody listens to a nobody until the nobodies unite and then they will command attention and can demand change'.

Forget anything to the contrary for it's nothing more than propaganda.

I have believed this for most of my life because having grown up in poverty in the small coal mining town of Amble in Northumberland and my dad being a miner who was off work frequently due to sickness, I had often witnessed the ignoring of those deemed by many to be of little significance.

I left school at the age of 15 years and carried out menial tasks until to the surprise of many me included, I was accepted into the police.

My roots never left me, and so I do know what it is like to be on the bottom rung of the ladder and overlooked. My humble start in life gave me an experience I have never forgotten and my desire to champion the underdog.

At the age now of 74, many have queried why at my age I bother. It's very simple, too many people accept a flawed world only because it is easier to do so than it is to try and change it. I am not one of them and I am not ready to give up on life yet!

The first thing I needed to do was to formulate a criterion for my new medal proposal.

Many of those in police circles said on hearing my plans, it will never happen because there are too many variants to consider in what the injury is and how it occurred. I never saw it that way and thought it was a simple matter to resolve.

Here is how I set my proposal out.

CLARIFICATION OF MY MEDAL PROPOSAL.

I've had a few queries as to the criteria of my medal proposal.

It is in fact very straightforward:

1) A police officer on duty.

2) Injured (defined as being of body or mind). So PTSD etc. is included.

3) Medically discharged from the service as a direct consequence of that injury.

That means the injured retiree will receive an additional 'injury on duty' (IOD) pension award.

To get the award the injury would have to be severe enough for the individual to be medically discharged from the service.

So, no 'IOD' award, no medal!

To be absolutely clear my proposal is in no way for a medal for bravery, heroism or 'gallantry'.

There are other medal awards already available for 'gallantry' BUT nothing for a posthumous or injury without it.

Most officers are deprived of an opportunity to show 'gallantry' because they are attacked instantly and without warning or sustain an injury in another way.

That is where the problem lies and why so many officers in the past 200 years have received no medal recognition whatsoever because the 'gallantry' bar is set so high for those available and without 'gallantry' nothing else is available, hence the important need to adopt my proposal.

My proposal is mainly directed towards those officers who were deprived ONLY by the injury of reaching the eligibility period for the LS & GC Medal, i.e. 20 years but before 2010 it was 22 years but reduced to 20 in line with the armed forces.

Now as I see it if an officer sustained injury and was medically discharged after receiving the LS & GC Medal, then he'd either receive my proposed medal additionally OR not.

The final decision on that will ultimately be made by the Government 'Honours' Committee' and so it is pointless concerning ourselves at this stage on that point.

My proposal will ensure no one, unless they leave of their own accord or are dismissed, would leave the service without a medal to wear at such times as Police Memorial Day.

Currently anyone severely injured and medically discharged, at such events would see their colleagues proudly wearing their LS & GC medal, whilst they could be mistaken for just another spectating member of the public with no connection to the Police Service, when in reality they have sacrificed so much health wise.

Many IOD's have sustained severe brain damage and/or are confined to wheelchairs, some requiring the services of an assistance dog.

We as a nation owe these poor folk more recognition than they receive now i.e. NOTHING!

The little I propose is nothing more than a substitute for those deprived ONLY through the sustained IOD of the LS & GC Medal.

I hope this clarifies my proposal BUT you need to be aware that I do not have the final say on this. It will be mulled over by MPs and finally the 'Honours' Committee' assuming the proposal gets that far.

I submit that without my proposal, the pending posthumous award, which a favourable announcement is expected on very soon, will undoubtedly cause problems. So, when the posthumous award is approved, as it is expected to be and issued retrospectively, then Sharon Beshenivsky will be a recipient.

However, without my proposal her colleague Teresa will again be overlooked. That cannot be allowed to happen!

It would be outrageous to award Sharon without Teresa because they attended the same incident, acting jointly and their actions were exactly the same.

My proposal will be presented to the House of Commons by my MP, Ms. Sally-Ann Hart MP for Hastings and Rye, who has pledged to do so.

Also, active and fully supporting my proposal is the Acting Deputy Speaker of the House, Sir Roger Gale MP.

I have already polled a sample of UK cross-party MPs and even prior to the presentation to the House, they have declared their support.

The House was unanimous in their support for the posthumous award and given that my proposal is so closely linked to that and the polled cross-party support, I would expect it to also be favourably received.

It's difficult to see how anyone can support an award for Sharon without a similar one for Teresa.

Acting on advice, I set up a public petition via change.org but that proved to be disastrous because after much hard work and the receipt of over 1,000 signatures, I found that any petition other than a Government one cannot be referred to in Parliament.

With that it was abandoned, and I was forced to begin from scratch again. How I regretted the loss of the hard fought for 1,000+ signatures, in that the great majority of signatories were unknown and therefore not contactable again. It takes a huge amount of time and effort to gain again the lost amount.

As a result of this, I then instigated the current parliamentary petition. The clock is ticking on its life because it is live for 6 months only. At 10,000 signatures, Government will respond to the petition and at 100,000 signatures, it will be considered for debate in Parliament.

I know it will not even get near the top figure and given the poor response so far, right now I have serious doubts that it will reach the lower.

It became clear to me that the key to success for the campaign would likely not lie with any petition. So, I came up with a plan of action. I believed that the answer might lie in the mass lobbying of MPs, and I set about organising that.

I was a member of several Facebook groups and in particular ones with police themes and retired police members. I appealed for volunteers to lobby their MP with a template email I formulated. However, I have to say the response was not encouraging to say the least. This came as somewhat of a surprise given what the subject matter was.

I found in the county I live, Sussex, there are 16 MPs and after a struggle, I gained someone to contact each one of them, some multiple times. The responses were different and some never did reply but a number did respond saying they would contact the Home Office.

I then contacted folks throughout the UK and requested they do the same to get a sample of the reaction.

The end result was that only a tiny amount of those MPs contacted even replied but there was enough to show there was positive cross-party support for my proposal. This was encouraging because it indicated the reaction the petition would receive from the House of Commons.

What was not so encouraging were the replies that came back via the

UK lobbied MPs from the Home office. It became apparent that there had been some collusion at the department. This was obvious when those who had lobbied their MP on my behalf forwarded to me the reply that their MP had received and passed on to the constituent from the department.

When comparing the responses, it was obviously a template letter had been churned out in response to any lobbied MP contacting them regarding my campaign. Only the name of the contacted MP was different.

This is what the template reply said:

Dear (MP's name), 2 October 2023

Thank you for your email of 4 September to the Home Secretary on behalf of your constituent Mr.............., regarding a petition to create a new medal to recognise officers who have been medically retired. I am responding as decisions regarding police medals fall under my remit as Permanent Secretary at the Home Office.

An official policing medal is a gift from the Government, on behalf of His Majesty the King to recognise individuals within the service. Medals can be awarded for long or meritorious service, or for cases of gallantry. There are also medals which can be awarded for specific events such as the coronation or jubilee celebrations of a monarch. The creation of a new medal requires a cross Government consensus before advice is put to HM The King, the implementation of a fair set of criteria and processes, and the allocation of funding.

We owe a tremendous gratitude to dedicated police officers for their continued hard work and sacrifice, not least in working hard during the recent two major Royal events to protect the public and the events. There is no doubt that police officers who have their service cut short have made, and in many cases will continue to make, an invaluable contribution to the emergency services. I would like to reassure your constituent that there are financial arrangements, through the pension and injury benefit schemes, that support police officers who are medically retired.

However, there are no plans to create a new medal specifically for this cohort. Though this will not be the response your constituent hoped for, I hope this clarifies the Government's position.

Yours sincerely,

Sir Matthew Rycroft KCMG CBE

Permanent Secretary

So, after contacting the Home Office regarding a proposal for a new medal to be created, the reply does not address that but goes on to patronise and tell what is available for gallantry and Coronation and Jubilee medals, none of which are relevant or even appropriate to a severely injured officer who has forfeited their job.

Prior to dismissal, the letter goes on to add insult to injury by referring to 'financial arrangements' when being requested to recognise the health sacrifice with a medal!

Well, you do not get much less sensitive and caring than that damned remark, do you! I compared it with saying, 'Why do you want a medal, we've given you a few extra quid!'

Imagine telling that to someone I know with 80% brain damage and confined to a wheelchair since being attacked in 1984!

SHAME on you Sir Matthew Rycroft KCMG CBE!

It seemed that we had hit the buffers and were not going to get any further with the approach to the Home Office. So, plan B had to be put into force.

I hit on an additional idea but to proceed with that I wanted an MP onboard with the best credentials in the UK to 'champion' the campaign and I recalled Sir Roger Gale MP for North Thanet (Kent).

Sir Roger has been an MP for about the last 40 years. He occupies what is considered a safe seat, but I believe that only to be because he is well thought of and respected by his constituents. He is currently the Acting Deputy Speaker for the House of Commons.

I first heard of and contacted Sir Roger over 30 years ago, when I heard that he was campaigning to restore capital punishment. I was of course a serving police officer then in Hastings, East Sussex and he was in the next county, Kent. I was impressed by his efforts for his campaign which I supported, and I wrote to him. Not being his constituent, I did not really expect a reply, but I did receive a very nice letter back.

Over the following years but not intentionally, I followed via the media some of his projects. I saw that at one stage he was on a parliamentary committee and accompanied police on their patrols. I am guessing he became interested in the work, and I was indeed surprised when in his 50s he joined the British Transport Police as a Special Constable.

Special Police Constable Roger Gale MP

Special Police Constable Roger Gale MP

Cynics may have thought it was only done as a self-promotional photo-shoot opportunity showing him in police uniform. They would have been proven wrong because he continued his duties for a number of years. How he got the time to do so along with being a very busy and conscientious MP I have no idea but admirably he did.

So, he more than adequately fitted my requirements as far as credentials were concerned. He was a law-and-order man being that he campaigned to restore capital punishment, and no one joins the Special Constabulary if they are anti-police. Him currently being Acting Deputy Speaker of the House, is a valuable further influential bonus I imagined.

I could not of course contact him directly in the hope of gaining his support. So, I made enquiries and recruited a very nice and willing former Kent police officer in his constituency, Mr Bob Pollard, to lobby him on my behalf. That was done and without requesting it, Sir

Roger on knowing what it was for made an appointment and I accompanied Bob.

I gave Sir Roger a very comprehensive briefing on my campaign proposal and without any hesitation he said he would act on it. I was delighted in that I'd got my chosen 'champion'. I would have travelled anywhere in the UK to seek his assistance and I considered it to be extremely fortunate that he was only situated in the adjoining county.

I brought the Home Office dismissal template letter to his attention and said I considered it to be insulting. Sir Roger said that he would speak with Chris Philp the Minister of State for Crime, Policing and Fire, and this he swiftly did. I received a copy of the letter he sent to Bob. I was encouraged to see that Sir Roger had told the Minister of State for Crime, Policing and Fire that he believed that the template response sent out en masse was 'unnecessarily dismissive'. I was delighted to read that because I thought it indicated that Sir Roger had stood up for what he believed was right and indeed for us against his colleagues. I was equally as pleased to hear that the minister had agreed to 'look at my proposal again'.

I consider that my efforts to seek out Sir Roger had proven worthwhile and that we had made a good start.

We all know the saying, 'It's not what you know but who you know', and here was an example confirming that to be so true. For when I first knew of the dismissal response from the Home Office, I wrote to the Minister of State for Crime, Policing and Fire, Chris Philp requesting an appointment to meet with him. The letter remains unacknowledged.

The Home Office U-turn also confirms my quote has credibility in that, 'Nobody listens to a nobody until the nobodies unite to command attention and then change can be demanded'. Well, we have not got the change we demand yet, but once deaf ears were beginning to listen.

I can reveal that the importance of the petition has only recently reduced because since Sir Roger became involved my once non-committal Hastings and Rye MP, Ms. Sally-Ann Hart, has now offered to present it to the House of Commons. Therefore, it should trigger a response from the Government without the need of the petition signatures reaching 10,000. That comes as a welcome relief.

One must wonder why Ms. Hart suddenly made her unsolicited offer because she had remained quiet up until then. Might I be termed a cynic to think it was because the Acting Deputy Speaker of the house was involved? Could it be that it suddenly had occurred to her that because the proposal had gained cross-party MP support it now looked likely to succeed? I believe many self-promoting MPs, in the same way as lawyers do, choose to link themselves to potential winning cases, which will enhance their own profile.

Here is the petition I have prepared for Ms. Hart to present to the House.

Petition: Recognition medal for injured police officers.

To the House of Commons.

The petition of Mr. Thomas William Curry and Jon Anthoni Cooper,

Declares that police officers in their effort to protect the public, are severely injured and are medically discharged from the service without the award of a medal recognition for their health sacrifice; further that the majority of officers, only through injury, are deprived of reaching the eligibility period to receive the police 'Long Service and Good Conduct Medal' and a substitute medal is needed; further that no such appropriate medal exists, other than if there are actions of 'gallantry', such as the George Cross, the George Medal, the King's Gallantry Medal and the King's Police Medal; and further that many police are attacked and injured and therefore not had the opportunity to display 'gallantry'.

The Petitioners therefore request that the House of Commons urge the Government to honour the Police Covenant by approving a new appropriate medal which recognises the health sacrifices of injured police officers.

And the petitioners remain, etc.

I set about busying myself in endeavouring to broadcast the campaign and the petition to solicit signatures via various Facebook groups I joined specifically for that purpose. I joined that many that every few days, I received a temporary and partial suspension from Facebook for being 'over-active' and so I was prevented from continuing my joining groups from time to time.

The periods were initially for 2 days at a time, but I just started up again as soon as the suspensions ended. The periods were eventually increased to 7 days. That tiny hiccup came to an end only when I had exhausted all of the appropriate groups to join. I must now be a member of 100s.

One of the groups I joined is called, 'British Police Long Service Medal Collectors' Club' and that is how I first had contact with the administrator of the site, a fine man by the name of Gordon Caldecott, a former North Wales police officer. Gordon had an inspirational idea and suggested that together we set up a new Facebook group, solely for the purpose of and duration of the campaign. I thought it was a brilliant idea and Gordon organised it and we became the two administrators.

We decided on calling the group, 'Campaign for Medal Recognition for Injured UK Police Officers'. In only 6 weeks the group gained 800 members and it continues to increase in numbers.

I shall be eternally grateful to Gordon for his fantastic and invaluable support.

CHAPTER 5

The POLICE FAMILY ADD INSULT TO INJURY

We now move to my biggest disappointment thus far. That being the negative reaction from many members of the so-called 'police family'. I had thought for many years that the frequent broadcasting of such a thing was grossly exaggerated but since the start of the campaign, more and more evidence of its virtual non-existence has emerged.

Many of those with police connections have failed to rally to my call to support the campaign for the benefit of our very own unfortunate severely maimed.

I have phoned and emailed repeatedly various police connections and associates without ever having had any response whatsoever. These include both county and National Police Federation Headquarters. After repeated attempts to make contact, I was eventually dismissed by Sussex Police Federation, Kent and Northumberland.

When I was eventually able to contact the Sussex Police Federation secretary, Andy Standing, I found him to be disinterested and after a very short time on the phone he said, 'I'll speak to our chairman', the chairman being Daren Egan.

I subsequently received the following email:

Sent: Monday, 21 Aug. 2023 at 15:17

Subject: RE: Petition proposal for special medal for police officers IOD.

'Good Afternoon, Tom.

As promised your Petition was discussed this morning during our meeting. As it stands at the moment, in its current form, we are unable to get behind this petition. I know this might be disappointing to you.

Kind Regards,

Andy.

Secretary

Sussex Police Federation. HQ'

I replied as follows:

'It's more than disappointing, it's shockingly stunning!... AND even more so because you do not think it appropriate to offer ANY explanation.

Whilst this is only your Sx. Branch, perhaps you can give me the contact details for the National Fed. HQ?'

I later sent this:

'Still no explanation of why the dismissal?

Surely it would be reasonable for me to expect a response as to why?'

He did provide me with an email address for National Police Federation HQ BUT I received no reply by way of explanation.

I suggest the non-reply indicates that there cannot be anything wrong with the 'current form' because everyone else seems satisfied with it and it has never changed from the beginning.

I compare his lack of response to that of a 'no comment' which I often got from a suspect when I had hit a nerve!

The Police Federation is supposed to be dedicated to ensuring the welfare of their members. However, I have to say the cavalier approach to welfare and care is beyond the realms of belief and staggeringly shameful from those who are in positions purporting to deliver that.

In my opinion, Messrs. Standing and Egan are to police welfare what the Chuckle Brothers were to comedy. Although come to think of it, the Chuckle Brothers were, on occasions, very funny and were nice guys. Seriously though, it is truly shocking and shameful of the Federation duo to have that disinterested attitude and whilst holding the positions they do.

So, these two serving police officers who are mere County Federation representatives block my path to reaching the National Federation HQ. The reason that they can do that is because HQ do not take phone calls or reply to emails if they are not via the County Federation office. What a ridiculous and flawed system, eh?

In August, I emailed the offices of the Sussex Chief Constable and the Police and Crime Commissioner (PCC) for Sussex. I was surprised when the next day the PCC, Katy Bourne, rang me. She listened patiently to my brief and very quickly said, "I will fully support your campaign." I told her about the snub from the two at the Sussex Federation and she said she would contact them. She did and sent me an email saying that the chairman, Daren Egan had said he would contact me. He never did even though I followed it up by emailing him and leaving voice mails. On the face of it, it would seem he lied to the PCC.

I was grateful to the PCC for her initial declaration of support but since then I have contacted her office and asked if she would contact all the other PCCs in the UK and bring the campaign to their attention. However, I have heard nothing at all back on that.

I have come to realise something and that is not to be too overjoyed when someone declares their 'full support'. That is, because to declare one's support and then to simply move on without doing anything further is not a true declaration of support but one of agreement only or perhaps, I dare say merely humouring.

One other thing I have learned is that when you do manage to make telephone contact, which is a rare occurrence, the vast majority of those in police circles and many others too, are always just on their way to a meeting. The rest of the time the phone is not answered. If you can leave a voice mail, it always seems to have not worked.

Emails have a problem too in that they simply could not be found.

I find this very strange in that what are all the meetings about? They could be contributing to the fact that nothing ever seems to be getting done.

How odd that we got to the moon in 1969 and yet everyday simple technology is forever failing especially that used by the police.

Now we move to Chief Constable Shiner. I first attempted to contact her office at the beginning of August. I tried to phone her office but got a voice message and I left a recorded request to contact me, and I emailed a few times, but no one contacted me.

If I ever get to meet with the Sussex Chief Constable, I'll ask her if she has ever considered changing her communications provider!

However, albeit a major part of the 'police family' are reluctant to support there are others of the same ilk.

There also seems to be a problem with the mail reliability too. I wrote to Chris Philp, the Minister of State for Crime, Policing and Fire, in

August but he could not have received my letter because he has not replied yet.

It's not good enough because the Royal Mail service is no better for the Royal family because also on 8 August 2023, I wrote to King Charles and Prince William appealing to them as ex forces members who will know the true value of medal recognition to show support. I also wrote to Princess Anne but all three could not have received my letters because as yet, I've had no replies. They might be forgiven because, whilst I am busy struggling with the 'police family' they have their family problems too.

However, at the beginning of September 2023, I did receive a reply from a member of the Royal Family and that was Princess Anne. I really expected her to tell me to 'Naff orf!' as she has told others in the past but to my surprise she did not.

This is what the reply letter said:

Buckingham Palace 1st September 2023

Dear Mr. Curry,

The Princess Royal has asked me to thank you for your letter dated 20th August concerning your proposal for the award of a new and special medal for members of the emergency services who have been injured and medically discharged from the service. Her Royal Highness read your letter with interest, but I am sure you will understand that The Princess is unable to intervene in the matters you raise as these are properly the concern of elected officials.

Thank you for taking the trouble to write and The Princess Royal sends her best wishes for the future.

Yours sincerely Anne Sullivan

Commander Anne Sullivan LVO Royal Navy Secretary to HRH The Princess Royal

---

Well, that was nice of Anne Sullivan to reply but goodness knows why she is opening and replying to Princess Anne's mail unless with her being an Anne too, they may often get their mail mixed up.

Anyway, I had a bit of luck in Anne Sullivan being ashore. She must have a second job when on shore leave to earn a bit of extra 'cash-in-hand' because maybe a sailor's wage might not be much to live on.

It was a nicely worded letter too from sailor Anne, but it says the same but more eloquently than what Princess Anne probably told her to say. I'm guessing that was, 'Tell him to naff orf!' Anyway it amounts to the same thing, eh?

When I wrote to HRH Princess Anne, I said that she would undoubtedly appreciate the importance of medal recognition and I gently reminded her of the kidnapping attempt on herself in The Mall in 1974.

This is what took place.

On 20 March 1974, 23-year-old Princess Anne, together with her first husband Captain Mark Phillips was returning to Buckingham Palace having attended a charity event.

As they drove along The Mall a white Ford car blocked their way, and suddenly its driver, Ian Ball, pulled out a handgun. Ball shot Anne's chauffeur, Alexander Callender and her police bodyguard, Inspector Jim Beaton. Ball was planning to kidnap the Princess for a £2 million ransom.

Beaton was shot three times, in the shoulder, hand and abdomen as he tried to protect the Princess.

Police Constable Michael Hills, 22, was first on the scene. Patrolling nearby, he heard sounds which alerted him, and he assumed the conflict was over a car accident. He approached Ball and the gunman shot him in the stomach.

Another motorist, named Glenmore Martin, had parked his car in front of the white Ford to keep Ball from escaping. Ball shot him.

Daily Mail journalist John Brian McConnell arrived at the scene. He said to Ball, "Don't be silly, old boy, put the gun down." Ball shot him and he fell. Now there were three injured men bleeding.

Ronald Russell was driving home from work when he saw the scene on the side of the road. He approached on foot after seeing Ian Ball confront Officer Hills.

Russell approached and punched Ball in the back of the head. While the former boxer distracted the gunman, Anne got out of the car. Ball ran towards her, but Anne jumped back into the vehicle. It was then that Russell punched him in the face. More police officers were now arriving and witnessed the action.

Peter Edmonds, a temporary detective constable, arrived at the scene and as he pulled up in his car, he saw a man run off with a gun through St. James's Park. Edmonds chased Ball, tackled him and made the arrest.

In total there were 5 men wounded, 2 police officers and 3 civilians. Beaton was shot three times and was triply lucky to survive. It surely was a narrow escape and how no one was killed was surely a miracle too.

Ian Ball pleaded guilty to attempted murder and a kidnapping charge. Sentenced to a life term in a mental health facility, he spent part of it at Broadmoor, a high-security psychiatric hospital.

In September, that year, Queen Elizabeth II awarded the George Cross, Britain's highest civilian award for courage, to Inspector Beaton. She presented the George Medal, the second highest civilian honour for bravery, to Police Constable Hills and Ronald Russell, and Queen's Gallantry medals (the third highest) to Police Constable Edmonds, John Brian McConnell and Alexander Callender. Glenmore Martin received the Queen's Commendation for Brave Conduct.

Given the harrowing experience and lucky escape Princess Anne had and the witnessing of 2 police officers being injured along with 3 members of the public, all in an effort to protect her, I would have thought she could have found some small way to support the campaign or at the very least commented.

Just when I'd stopped thinking about receiving any further replies from the Royal Family, on 8 December 2023, 10 weeks after writing to him, Prince William's office replied. Here's what the letter said:

Kensington Palace

Dear Mr Curry, 8 December 2023

I am writing to thank you for your letter to The Prince of Wales outlining your suggestions for a special medal to be awarded to members of the emergency services who have been medically discharged from service.

His Royal Highness always appreciates receiving the views of individuals, and you can rest assured that your comments have been very carefully noted. If you have not done so already, you may wish to contact The Minister of State for Crime, Policing, and Fire about this matter.

It was thoughtful of you to take the trouble to write as you did. The Prince of Wales would have me send his best wishes.

Yours sincerely,

Head of Royal Correspondence.

I had already written to the Minister of State for Crime, Policing and Fire mentioned in the letter back in August. The letter went unacknowledged, but it is now irrelevant because Sir Roger Gale MP is in discussions with him.

So, another non-supportive but polite get lost letter. There is one more reply from the King awaited, if I get a reply.

I didn't bother writing to Prince Andrew because he loves company, and he might be busy with all his mates!

Loads of other people must have trouble with emails too because many MPs have not replied. Here's but a few: Rishi Sunak, Suella Braverman (we'll forgive her because she'll be busy job hunting), Sir Kier Starmer and Ed Davey. You'd think the last two would have replied because they'll be out and about touting for votes soon at election time.

I recruited obliging volunteers from all over the UK to lobby their MP, about 100 in total. I'd guess about 75% did not reply to their constituents. Out of the other 25'ish about 15 missed the point totally and went off on a patronising ramble ending with, 'Thank you for contacting me'. Maybe they just thought folks contacted them because they only wanted a pen pal!

The exercise was not a total waste of time because out of the 10'ish who did respond, it showed cross-party support from, Conservatives, Labour, Liberal Democrats, Welsh Labour, SNP, UK Independence Party and Green Party in that they positively declared their support and as my template letter requested, they obliged by declaring their support to Sir Roger and Sally-Ann.

On the positive side, no MP has ever said, 'I do not support the campaign'.

This is a welcome sign because when the posthumous award proposal went to the House of Commons the support was unanimous. Given that my proposal is so closely linked to the posthumous medal award proposal and the sample of UK cross-party polled support, I cannot see there being any different reaction to my proposal for the injured.

My information at this moment (8 December 2023) is that the

posthumous award proposal is with King Charles for his approval. I submit that it is unlikely that the King will not approve any proposal reaching him from his Government. Chris Philp, the Minister of State for Crime, Policing and Fire, said only recently, 'an announcement is expected soon'. When it is it will greatly enhance the chance of my proposal receiving approval too.

As many doors refused to open, I hatched various plan B's.

I recalled my police days and back then it was part of my job to break down barriers to get to the ultimate prize, normally the villain. I thought then it was no good barricading the front door to keep me out if they forgot to secure the back door.

So, I set myself a challenge to find a back door for those who snubbed me and my campaign!

In mid-September, I contacted the senior reporter for the Worthing Herald (part of the Sussex News Group), Sam Morton. Sam agreed to include an article in the news on my campaign.

Not having heard from the Chief Constable's office, I hit on a devious plan. I asked Sam to contact the Chief Constable for a quote, and he said he would. I knew it was likely the Chief would not even be aware of any campaign but after being approached by a newspaper reporter, would certainly then want to.

Well, that afternoon my phone rang and 'blow me down' guess who it was? It was the Chief Constable's staff officer, Chief Inspector Paul Nellis, who was full of profuse apologies for not being in contact earlier. This was due to staffing problems etc. he said. He said he'd like to know a bit more about the campaign. He said his phoning me that day was purely coincidental and nothing whatsoever to do with my friendly 'newshound sniffing about'. Yeah, right!

I can probably guess exactly what happened. The reporter caused panic and stirred the instant reaction. My tactic had worked a treat. I had my own thoughts and suspicions, but I kept them to myself. I'll leave you to form your own opinion but 'coincidences' are always the last thing I consider!

I was just happy that I'd found a way of reaching the Chief Constable via the back door!

On 23 October, Sam Morton, as promised, delivered a great article which was circulated throughout Sussex. It was a pity it was not nationally because I got no interest from the tabloids, but it was a helpful start at least. In the piece there was a photograph of the Chief Constable and this statement: 'Sussex Police also confirmed that Chief Constable Jo Shiner has received correspondence from Mr. Curry and is looking forward to hearing more when she meets with him'.

However, Ms. Shiner cannot be too enthusiastic to meet with me, for the appointment was made for 4 January 2024. I tried repeatedly to gain an earlier one without success. I was told the Chief Constable was busy and her diary was full. That will be over four months since I first contacted her office. It's worrying that a chief constable does not give precedence to an issue concerning the maiming of her officers and it takes over four months to meet with me, especially as it was said that she's looking forward to hearing more when she meets me. Is that not an astoundingly long wait given the subject matter? It certainly does not appear to be high on the Chief Constable's priority list. Maybe that goes some way to explaining why this has taken 200 years to get started and only with my forcing it.

I decided I would keep the appointment but the Chief Constable's relevance to my struggle to get the campaign started is now less important being that things have swiftly and positively progressed. Any support she will be able to give would have been more helpful at the beginning and not so much of a value now that it is underway and indeed gaining in momentum.

I have spoken again with Mr. Nellis the Chief Constable's staff officer, and I told him about the two Federation representatives and their disinterest. I was told the Chief Constable has no control over them. What! A chief constable has no control over her own junior officers? No wonder they can do what they want in terms of not being easy to contact and can do as they please if they are not answerable to the highest senior officer within their force. Phew!

As of the 9 December 2023, the National Police Federation are not involved, unlike the posthumous medal award campaign, which they most certainly are supporting.

Equally disappointingly, I got the same negative and dismissive response from the CEO of the National Association of Retired Police Officers (NARPO), Mr. Alan Lees, as I had from the Federation. Mr. Lees also appeared disinterested and failed to offer any support whatsoever.

On the 8 August 2023, he sent an email and here is part of the content:

'As you are aware, Police officers need to meet the criteria set by the Royal Warrant for the 'Long Service and Good Conduct Medal'.

On leaving the Police, officers receive a Certificate of Loyal Service. In addition, Police officers also can receive medals to recognise their service, such as the Silver, Golden and Platinum Jubilees and the Coronation. Therefore, there are ways to recognise service, which will include those who retired injured on duty and on ill-health retirement, not necessarily awarding a separate medal.'

Surprisingly, he appeared to have little understanding of the problem and indeed by not requesting further information, did not appear to want any either. It's clear he thought he knew it all.

There was no need whatsoever for his reference to the inappropriate certificate and medals in his first paragraph, after all, that was why there was a need for my campaign. He seemed to think a 'Certificate of Loyal Service' was relevant. Perhaps he was suggesting that the certificate could be pinned to the chest of the injured denoting their sacrifice, at such events as Police Memorial Day.

His referencing Jubilee and Coronation medals is equally as irrelevant. For a start not all officers received them, for example if you did not serve during the eligible period. The only one I did serve during was the Silver Jubilee BUT that was the only Jubilee medal that was not issued to everyone serving at that time. Only 30,000 medals were struck, and they were only issued to nominated recipients. I was not one of the nominated and so I did not receive it.

It's disconcerting to say the least that the CEO of NARPO does not have any true understanding of the medal situation. I was one too who left the service without a medal of any description and so that shoots his argument down in flames immediately.

In any case, the medals he refers to have no relevance other than to indicate an officer served at that time. To suggest a mere Jubilee medal is in any form an appropriate substitute for being deprived, due to no fault of your own, of a LS & GC Medal and only through being severely injured is laughable. It is comparable to that of saying to someone in a wheelchair, 'Never mind you've got your Tufty Club badge, wear that'! Eventually, after trying repeatedly to get through to the lacking in empathy Mr. Lees I had to admit defeat and move on.

Thinking that normally everyone is answerable to someone and even the King is answerable to his Government, I thought who is Alan Lees answerable to then?

So, I approached the Southeast Regional NARPO National Executive Committee (NEC) representative, Mr. Ahmed Ramiz, who patiently and compassionately heard my full argument. He instantly said, "I personally will support the campaign." He then offered to present it at the next NEC meeting, which he did, and the committee wisely and unanimously agreed to support my proposal.

My grateful thanks and appreciation go to the willing Ahmed and to the NEC for their support. The NEC is the NARPO CEO's boss, and so now the reluctant Mr. Lees would have no option other than to do as he was told by NEC.

That was another back door by which I gained entry to NARPO HQ. Now they may have also handed me the key to the back door of the National Police Federation. Certainly, by NARPO now supporting the campaign, it does in police circles add a degree of credibility to my proposal.

NARPO have now finally circulated my proposal to ALL 106 UK branch secretaries who may but are not obliged to forward it to their respective members. It was circulated to the branch secretaries on Friday 24 November 2023.

My own fully supportive Eastbourne branch secretary, the highly efficient Kevin Moore, forwarded it on to his members instantly.

This was not the same reaction from the majority of the others. As of this moment, some still have not forwarded it to their branch members. Whether they will or not remains to be seen. What is apparent is that there are many within police circles who believe the campaign is undeserving of any additional attention or urgency above and beyond any other everyday matter.

Just as an example, the secretary for Brighton said he will circulate it within his Christmas newsletter. That indicates a casual approach as opposed to prioritising something of such relevance and to support injured members of the so-called 'police family'.

Disappointingly, as in many other matters in life, too many appear to be of the opinion of 'If it does not include me, then I'm not interested'. The circulation to all 90,000 members of NARPO, has led to no noticeable increase in the petition signatories or those joining our Facebook group. This confirms my theory of there being no such thing as a 'police family'.

As of 9 December, petition signatures stood at a paltry 2,204. A petition to keep a village Post Office garner far more than that and this is for a national campaign to seek medal recognition for severely maimed retired police officers.

I do not believe that the campaign will fail because of low petition signature numbers or without the Federation being onboard. In this case I have MPs willing to present the petition and a most prominent and respected 'champion'. If that were not the case the petition numbers would be crucial because if there are less than 10,000 signatures, then the petition is useless. However, the signature numbers on the petition will be disclosed at the same time as the petition is presented and I really do not want the figure to look low and thereby appear to lack support.

There is a six months' time limit for a petition. We are now into the 3rd month so with only 2,204 it's not looking good. Sadly, as I have already bombarded Facebook groups with it, I've run out of options.

Anyway, it's in the hands of the Government and that is looking encouraging. At the end of the day, if the Government say, 'You are having it', then in this instance what the Federation want is totally irrelevant but still I'd rather see them support it than not.

I have also directly encountered the disinterest and apathy from former uninjured police officers. I have had contact with many via various Facebook groups and I have been frequently disappointed by their reaction and reluctance to take mere seconds to sign the petition. It's so simple to click on the link add your name, postcode and email address and it's then completed.

I know now to accept defeat when I'm told, 'I'm busy, I'll do it later'. I'll guarantee when that is said, their signature will never be added to the petition.

CHAPTER 6

THE SKULDUGGERY OF THE SUSSEX PPA

Up to now there has been much mention of bad treatment of IOD's and skulduggery by the PPA's. As unbelievable as it may sound to some as far as I am concerned, I believe they are capable of all that has been related and much more and I have been a victim of it at its worst.

I will now give the details of my shocking experience and the depths that many Police Pensions Authorities (PPA) will go to seize back monies paid to injured police officers. The facts I will refer to are stunning in their callousness and corruption and of those who seek to ingratiate themselves through the skulduggery of fraudulent methods to cost save and reduce pressure on budgets.

After my life-changing injury in 1989, I had been retired and in receipt of my injury pension award for two years, when in 1991, I received a demand from Sussex PPA for a 5-figure sum plus a daily amount of interest over the past two years. This was a significant amount of money and caused me and my wife of the time a great deal of worry.

The claim was made and based on an historical and technical clause, of which neither the PPA nor I were aware of. The only way the PPA found out about it was by some wise guy contacting the Home Office to seek advice as to whether it was possible for the PPA to use the technicality to claw back monies from genuine recipients.

The Home Office indicated that it might be, but it was very technical and such a move had to be the PPA's decision as to whether they proceeded or not. That was good enough for them and they went on the attack. Later and by using the Freedom of Information Act, I found out about the request from the Home Office and my argument was then based on, 'how do you expect me to know IF the PPA does not, and they are the ones who advise me of the regulations?'

So, the other 160 plus IOD recipients in Sussex all got the demand letters at the same time blaming them for what they described as an overpayment. In fact, it was far from an overpayment it was a technical claim on a normal payment. The claim was unjust, and I was not going to compliantly submit to their unlawful refund demand. However, as far as I know, I was the only one who refused to repay the monies. The others agreed and began to repay in instalments.

I sought assistance/support from a Sussex Police Federation representative, a PC Fox, who said to me, 'We can't support you because you are not a copper anymore'. The dismissive PC Fox even refused to supply me with a copy of the police pension regulations. I now know that the Federation should have supported me because I was still a police officer at the time of the award and the monies argued over were the same going forward into retirement.

It was at a time prior to my being able to access computers and the only way I could get a copy was to drive to Brighton University and obtain the information from their vast library which I did.

NARPO said, 'We agree with you BUT we do not have the funds to support you'. I found that strange because part of their motto at the time was, 'to safeguard pensions', but that bit has been dropped now I believe. As for a shortage of funds, I saw individuals attending conferences and staying at good UK hotels accompanied by their wives. I also heard from reliable sources of fancy meals being consumed and free drinks. Recently a source from within NARPO when I had cause to mention this said the wives were always paid for by the member they were accompanying. I still have doubts as to why when it is normally only ever a 2-day conference and supposed to be a working time, the need for wives to be there. It still smacks of a free short stay to me.

So, abandoned by both the Federation and NARPO, for the following two years, I busied myself preparing my defence, EVEN THOUGH I WAS ILL!

The PPA tried everything in trying to force me into paying, for example, saying, 'If you lose our costs could be in the region of £30,000 in addition to that claimed'.' My ex-wife showed no support (but neither did anyone else agree with me) saying, "It's the police and they wouldn't do it if it wasn't right, and you say you know better than them? You are going to lose us this house!" I said, "I know what's right and, in this case, they are not." We argued a lot.

I knew that two years before I was medically discharged, 1987, I had been issued with a 43-page pension scheme guidance booklet by the Sussex PPA (as was every other Sussex serving officer) and me being careful and organised, I still had it. I checked it and on page 13 of the book, there is short sentence which was VERY relevant to the PPA's claim of refund. The sentence states:

'The injury pension is then reduced by any DSS benefit payable in respect of the injury'.

Back then DSS was the Department of Social Security and what is now the Department of Works and Pensions.

That was the part that the PPA was basing their claim on. However, I had never received ANY payment from the DSS for my injury. So, what was it that the PPA were trying to claim the refund on? I could not see how they had any form of claim, and I was confused. I had no one to seek advice from as I was not going to go down the route of paying 1000s for a defence lawyer and I trusted my own judgement and capability AND I do not frighten easily.

I continued my research, and I discovered a 'stated case' relevant to my case. A stated case is when a judgement is made in a high court in a particular case and is then referenced in any identical future cases. It ensures uniformity in court rulings from then on. The stated case was one of a pension authority versus a retired teacher and the ruling was as follows: 'If any monies are paid erroneously by a payee and neither the recipient nor the payee knew, then any overpayment cannot be claimed retrospectively'.

So, there we have it, even if there had been any overpayment AND there had not been any such thing (you recall I said that I had received nothing from the DSS for my injury) the PPA cannot claim the monies back retrospectively.

I made the PPA aware of the stated case, but they disregarded it. I felt confident now, but they must have thought by holding out I would submit prior to the threatened court hearing date. That was just not going to happen!

My preparations continued and I decided I needed to acquire at least 3 more copies of the pension booklet I was given whilst still serving. I needed them to reference on the day of the hearing, one for me, the judge, prosecuting lawyer and any witness.

I asked my former colleagues if they still had theirs but not being as methodical as me, it proved difficult, and I was only ever able to acquire one other. I was supplied with it from a friend, who said, "It's not my original copy because I mislaid that, but I was able to get a replacement a few years later." Little did I know at the time how significant that statement would prove to be!

Now having possession of the new booklet, I was referencing it and I spotted something different and odd. I saw that the name of the Sussex PPA treasurer was different to that shown in my copy. In mine it was Fieldhouse but in my former colleague's it was Rigg. This set-off alarm bells! I gave it my full attention and scrutinised the whole booklet in minute detail. The print dates were the same, 1987 BUT that could not be so because the treasurer's names were different and Rigg was not the treasurer until much later. I was on to something here because the print dates could not both be 1987! It was obvious that there had been a re-print BUT the re-print date was not amended. Why?

I guessed why and I shot to page 13. The sentence that I previously referred to had been altered to read:

'The injury pension is then reduced by any relevant DSS benefit whether or not related to the injury', which is so much different to that stated in my original copy.

The only part of the 43-page booklet that had been altered apart from the give-away treasurer's name was the sentence relative to mine and others' demanded refund. So, it was undeniable proof that the booklet had, in my opinion, been fraudulently altered to entrap we recipients and only to bring about a refund. I would argue that this amounts to criminality at its finest, eh?

Let me just print again and alongside one another the two sentences so they can easily be compared. The first is from my original booklet and the second is from my former colleague's copy:

1). 'The injury pension is then reduced by any DSS benefit payable in respect of the injury'.

2). 'The injury pension is then reduced by any relevant DSS benefit whether or not related to the injury'.

They were actually after my 'DSS sickness benefit' and not the totally separate 'DSS injury benefit' which I had never received.

Now I was prepared for the day of the court hearing.

Damning as my gathered evidence was, the PPA continued to demand the monies and merely dismissed any references I made to either the stated case or the skulduggery of the unrecorded re-print date and 'amendment', as being totally irrelevant. They were in my opinion either desperately bluffing or fools, or a combination of both, but either way these individuals representing the PPA were going to proceed regardless!

I wanted the then NARPO secretary, Alec Faragher, to attend court to confirm he had said that he agreed with me, but he said that NARPO would not allow him to attend a court to give evidence in a case that he'd had nothing to do with.

I had also requested a close friend and former colleague, PC Roy Millar, who was still serving at Hastings police station, to attend to give evidence in my favour and additionally as a character witness. His evidence was to be that as a local Federation representative he had never heard of any such pension regulation that allowed such an unwarranted demand of a refund and that he supported my defence. Roy had been willing to attend. However, closer to the court date, he said the police were not approving his attendance.

I had other ideas regarding my two potential witnesses, and I subpoenaed both of them. I squared it beforehand with the lovely Roy. It meant the police had no option but to allow him to attend. I even arranged for his appearance to be on one of his rest days, so he got paid the overtime rate!

Eventually, the court hearing date arrived. I donned my suit and gathered my unsupported, self-generated but damning defence papers and headed for the court.

At the court, I saw Mr. Trott, solicitor for the Sussex PPA, who I'd had dealings with previously and an appointed barrister. Roy and the reluctant Alec were not there but their attendance would be required the next day.

Even as I entered the courtroom door, Paul Trott was still trying to persuade me to submit. He said, "Offer us anything a month and we might be able to accept." I said, "How about nothing? I have the two books and we'll go ahead, eh?" I held the two books up for him to see and contemplate.

So, an ill son of a Northumbrian coal miner who left a pit village with basic school education at the age of 15 without any academic qualifications to his name, entered the court to present his defence up against a Queen's Counsel barrister. A Geordie speaker versus a plum in the mouth well educated man. Truly a David and Goliath tale, one might view it as.

The case opened and it was soon clear to me that they had nothing to support their claim. I had much in my defence. The evidence of them being so unsure of their ground that they sought advice from the Home Office before their premeditated attack on the unsuspecting and naive injured was launched, the case stated and the two contradictory and evidentially damning booklets.

Let me share what I think is the only humorous moment of this shameful tale. The PPA barrister not having much to go on and looking a little shaky, endeavoured as best he could to paint a bad picture of my character. He presented something to the judge, by means of a statement from a Mr. Saunders, from the Sussex PPA office. I had accepted the statement to be entered as evidence without the need for the witness to appear because I saw no relevance and viewed it as being dumb and unimportant in proving any guilt on my behalf. In fact, I thought it was a pathetic and desperate attempt to demean me but achieved nothing of any real significance.

The statement from Mr. Saunders read as follows:

'On ....I took another phone call from Mr. Curry who was again angry and upset. I told him that he had three options to settle the outstanding amount, 1. Forfeit all his pension until it was paid in full. 2. Pay £500 a month until it was paid or 3. Go before an arbitrary judge for an independent decision on how much to pay each month. Mr. Curry said, "What about option 4?" I said, "What is option 4?" Mr. Curry said, " You can go and .... yourself because you are not getting a penny!"

The judge looked at me and said, "Is that what you said?" I said, "Yes, sir and that is why I agreed to accepting the statement from Mr. Saunders without his attendance." He said, "Why did you say that?" I said, "Because they had no right to it, and I wasn't going to pay." The judge said to the prosecuting barrister, "Carry on Mr. ...."

The barrister then related something else it was alleged I had done, as follows:

I'd had many dealings over the two preceding years, with both Mr. Saunders and Mr. Trott and I had repeatedly asked when the threatened court hearing would be. On the first-year anniversary of the beginning of our farcical dealings, I sent them an anniversary card. It depicted two teddy bears sat at opposite ends of a bath. I'd written on the chest of one, Saunders and on the other, Trott. Printed on the front of the card were the words, 'Everything changes over the years' and when it was opened it read, 'until it comes to you two'. I'd seen it when shopping for another greetings card and I just could not resist it.

After the barrister presented it, the judge once again addressed me and asked, "Did you send the card?" I said, "Yes I did, sir." He said, "Why?" I said, "Because it was the first-year anniversary since we'd began our dealings." I noted a slight glimmer of a smile from the judge as he said, "Carry on, Mr. ...."

Shortly it was my turn to present my defence evidence. I said, "I'm sure Your Honour will be aware that there is a stated case relevant to this case. If it is helpful, I can supply you with a copy of it?" One thing was certain, he had no idea there was a relevant stated case, but he merely said, "Thank you," and I handed it over.

Just as I was about to reference the two contradictory booklets, some whispering took place between Mr. Trott and the barrister. I was then surprised that just as I was getting into my stride, the barrister addressed the judge and requested that the case be adjourned for three weeks so he might seek further instructions. The judge agreed and before he left the courtroom, he said, "I will agree to the adjournment but in doing so I do hope that an agreement is reached in good time to avoid this case re-opening." I thought that was a clear signal to the PPA to re-think their decision.

Three days before the adjourned court date, I received a letter from the Sussex PPA. What it said is imprinted in my memory so much so I can quote its contents word for word. It said:

'Dear Mr. Curry, As we have no desire for an acrimonious argument with one of our own, it has been decided to withdraw the court proceedings against yourself. We apologise for any inconvenience'.

Well how very nice and considerate of them, eh? It was strange though that they were willing to enter an acrimonious argument with me for the past two years. I know exactly why they halted the case. It was because knowing I was unrepresented and they had a fancy barrister they thought that at the last minute when it dawned on me that they were proceeding, I would 'bottle' and make an offer and that this had back-fired.

They also knew that I had only been a PC of no great importance or standing, and along with my northeast dialect, my 'go and.... yourself' and teddy card, that I would be a pushover. It had all, I believe, wrong-footed them into making the first mistake of warfare and that is to 'Never underestimate your enemy'. I tried to adhere to the second of, 'Never correct your enemy when he's making a mistake'.

There were two other happy folks, Roy and NARPO Alec and especially the relieved, Alec. Roy on hearing the news and being a careful Scot said, "Aye, but yer no havin' the attendance money back though!" I had to pay that when I applied for the subpoena. I allowed him to retain that, and we shared a drink on the strength of it. The rest of the so- called 'police family' could just not understand why the tough Scot, Roy, was still such a close friend of a guy who had subpoenaed him. We frequently laughed about that together. Sadly, Roy is no longer with us, and I greatly miss him being about.

Alec at NARPO asked if I'd agree to him circulating the full story to all the UK members as a warning in their magazine as it was of such great importance. I willingly agreed.

This article was published by NARPO in the Quarterly Bulletin No. 147 Summer1993:

OVERPAYMENT CASES.

Instances continue to occur of Police Authorities seeking to recover monies, apparently overpaid to Police Pensioners.

Police Regulations are such that any monies being received from DSS in respect of the 'relevant injury' (the injury responsible for medical discharge and pension) are deductible from the injury pension. Here is a complication in that, if benefit is continued from employment to pension without a break, then any DSS monies received for whatever reason (even a common cold) are deductible from the injury pension. The advice to such persons is, therefore, to break the continuity of the sickness for a period, by applying for unemployment benefit or obtaining employment.

In 1991 the Treasurer's Department of the Sussex Police Authority discovered that they had been erroneously making pension payments to Police Pensioners who had been discharged on medical grounds as a result of injuries received in the course of their duties. In an attempt to recover such monies, they sought to obtain signatures to a document which would commit those signing to the repayment of any overpayment. There were quite a large number of pensioners involved and the distressing feature of the document sent was that it failed to inform the recipients of the error - which was that of the Treasurer's Department - or of their intention in the issuing of the document.

The NEC office was informed in 1992 of the approach to all pensioners to repay the monies mistakenly overpaid.

There was a High Court decision, Avon County Council v. Howlett in 1983, which is the decided case to use in such instances. The Court decision concerns itself with mistakes of fact or mistakes of law by paying authorities leading to the overpayments.

Monies overpaid by mistakes of law are not recoverable whilst those overpaid by mistake of fact - whilst recoverable - can be contested by claiming 'Estoppel'. This briefly means that if the person in receipt of the payment either was unaware of the payments or believed he was entitled to them and spent the monies then the authority could not recover the money.

The (then) General Secretary of NARPO, Alec Faragher, made representations, and as a result the Sussex Police Authority Treasurer's Department recognised that, in most cases, the monies could not be reclaimed, and those pensioners were so informed. That same department however, decided to pursue those who had signed the document and decided to make a test case of one pensioner, a Tom Curry, who had, by the error, been overpaid a large sum. There was an inference of dishonesty or deceit by non-disclosure of information, but it must be emphasized that the overpayments made were not known at the time by either Mr Curry or any of the others involved.

Assistance in this matter was sought through the Police Federation and we wish to acknowledge the help given in this matter and in all the instances where matters of principle are involved. Legal advice was given by the Federation solicitors who, on this occasion, recommended that the matter should not be pursued on behalf of Mr Curry.

Alec however, persisted with this matter basing his argument on two main points. If it was a mistake in law, in that the Police Regulations had been wrongly interpreted for many years, then there was no recovery process.

If it was an error of fact, then Mr Curry had been misinformed in documents supplied to him, had not concealed anything, and believed he was fully entitled to the monies which he had spent as part of his everyday outgoings.

A summons was duly issued against Mr Curry, who in turn, issued subpoenas to ensure the attendance of certain witnesses - including Alec Faragher - a date was set for the hearing.

Approximately two weeks before the hearing Mr Curry was advised that the Sussex Police Authority was reluctant to pursue a long and acrimonious argument in open court against one of its pensioners.

It would have been far easier, less costly and more pleasant if that attitude had been displayed in 1991, rather than when it was apparent that the case would not be successful.

Tom Curry and his family have suffered over two years, as a result the Sussex Police Authority who saw fit to wield the big guns on this issue, apart from the possible inference there has been against his character.

The withdrawal by them from the case does not indicate compassion but can be laid most definitely at the door of Alec Faragher who by his tenacity and strength of purpose beat them. We all owe him a debt of gratitude.

The article was not factual and not what I had anticipated. It seemed that NARPO had fully supported and won the day for me. That was not true, only one guy did that and at the risk of financial ruin - Tom Curry!

If Alec and NARPO had been so willing, why did I need to subpoena him? The article was written by Alec and claimed far more credit for himself, NARPO and the Federation than that due and our versions of events differ greatly.

However, I was so relieved it was all successfully behind me that I overlooked the NARPO advantageous indiscretion. After all, in the scheme of things it was of no consequence.

I believe the case had been halted for two main reasons. 1) The exposure and repercussions of what I believe to be the stunningly reckless criminality of the fraudulent re-printing of the booklet. 2) The impact had the case continued and undoubtedly been found in my favour would be that all those IOD pensioners, who had begun to repay would have had all their money refunded.

However, this way if any one of the 160 plus referenced my case, they would be told, 'He didn't win, the case was withdrawn, and we cannot discuss any individual'.

I ask that you note the premeditated and devious action, prior to disclosure of the intention to demand the refund, by requesting ALL to sign the document stating any overpayments would be repaid. This was only done after the Sussex PPA had thought of and planned their demand and had sought advice from the Home Office. Initially the document was solely intended to be used and quoted specifically in this instance. I recall the wording was that 'any overpayment will be repaid irrespective of who is responsible for the error'. It also stated that 'refusal to sign may incur the withholding of the pension award'.

This was clearly an unlawful threat and cunningly designed to manipulate around the lawful rights of the recipient. I compare this with that of forcing the signing of a contract with one's arm up the back. I'm sure that no court would uphold or indeed condone such behaviour. However, I guarantee that the vast majority of recipients will have been reminded of the document. In naivety and having been instigated by a thought to be reputable and trustworthy PPA, those reminded would have believed it to be a lawful contract and would have submitted to the unwarranted demand. I submit this action alone was totally illegal entrapment!

IF the individual who ordered the re-print had not slipped up by making the mistake of putting Rigg's name in as being the treasurer at the time this was done, then they likely would have gotten away with it undetected. However, irrespective of that they could not have avoided and beaten the stated case that existed and fortunately I discovered it and in time too.

Since 1989, my forced injury retirement has been blighted by the continual harassment of the PPA, purely for the purpose of seizing back my injury award. They are entitled for the rest of my life as and when they choose, to medically review my award. At the age of 74 and 34 years since I left the police and with little chance of my health improving now, wouldn't you think I'd earned the right for some peace of mind and to be left alone? The answer is, no, it's not to be!

That is why I keep safe and closely guard the security of the two booklets, kept in my possession as future insurance and to corroborate my harassment claims.

I relate my shocking experience only to support my claims of there being no such thing as a 'police family' and that wrongdoings do occur involving the injured and their pensions. My research reveals the whole of the UK is rife with dishonourable treatment in regard to IOD pension awards and towards those undeserving of such a lack of compassion.

My account is not an isolated one and there are far too many similar, many where injured officers are simply deviously outmanoeuvred by PPAs and deprived of their deserved injury award.

Many involved are vulnerable with PTSD or a brain injury, such as poor Angie McLoughlin who you have already read about. These folks will be putty in the hands of those who seek to manipulate and take advantage of them.

There is little sympathy or care for those who miss out on recognition and a medal BUT there is none whatsoever when it comes to money and budgets!

Police pension maladministration is a huge minefield, and the poison chalice is way above my remit and capabilities.

Incompetence and skulduggery, at its most extreme and from a PPA!

NOTE. If any reader has any doubts as to the validity of my account in this chapter, please remember that you are reading it in a published book and any libelous statement could result in court action, of which I am fully aware.

Sussex PPA be conscious of the fact that even after 35 plus years, I still have the two conflicting and what I believe are fraudulent booklets!

CHAPTER 7

THE CAMPAIGN STRUGGLE CONTINUES

Back in September 2023, I had tried other police connected representative groups thinking that if I could recruit their support my campaign would reach the ears of the National Federation and they would finally realise that my proposal had merit. However, all my considerable efforts were thwarted by either not acknowledging my approach or through disinterest.

Here is a list and result of my efforts:

1). 20 August 2023 Metropolitan Police Commissioner. Emailed. No reply.

2). 7 September 2023 National Police Memorial Day. Emailed. No reply.

3). 7 September 2023 Disabled Police Association. Emailed. No reply.

4). 7 September 2023 Disability in Policing. Rachel. Emailed. No reply.

5). 7 & 29 September 2023 Black Police Association, Simon Miah, Essex. Emailed. No reply.

6). 25 September 2023 Superintendents' Association, Paul Fotheringham. Emailed and spoke on phone. He said he'd passed it on. No reply.

7). 25 September 2023 Disability Reserve Place. Supt. Paul Burrows. Nottinghamshire Police. Emailed. No reply.

8). 25 September 2023 British Transport Police. (BTPFED). Emailed and spoke on phone several times with Pete Kingham, board member. He said he'd passed it on. No reply.

9). 11 October 2023 NARBTPO (National Association for Retired British Transport Police Officers). Text and voice mailed. No reply.

10). 6 November 2023 Scottish Police Federation David Kennedy (Secretary). I spoke to him on the phone. He initially declared support. He later said he'd spoken with the National Federation, and they had said something was pending as second string to the 'posthumous award'. This is not so. Since then, I have emailed him. The Home Office have corroborative proof of no other pending campaign. I left voice messages with corroborative evidence negating his statement. Mr. Kennedy is now elusive.

I think you will have the general idea by now of the apathy and disinterest displayed by those who profess to and are paid to support the welfare of police officers. I think it is high time they were exposed, named and shamed!

Thinking that the mayors of London and Greater Manchester might be interested I emailed them both. Given that many police officers have been killed and maimed in their large cities in recent times, I was disappointed by their disinterest and dismissal.

I also emailed numerous Police connected charities, i.e., Thin Blue Line, Cops, David Rathband Foundation, Matt Ratana Foundation etc. However, nothing resulted from any of the contact.

I could carry on with the list of dismissals but rather than this book ending up competing with the telephone book, I believe I've made my point and will leave it at that. You may understand now why I thought the communication systems for all police connections had crashed!

I wish to move on now and reference a group that many of my former police injured colleagues have mentioned. The Injury on Duty Pensioners' Association (IODPA). I was a member of this group and when the membership stood at only 400, I endeavoured to increase it by emailing individually every single one of the 106 NARPO branch secretaries in the UK, requesting that they broadcast the existence of IODPA.

The three trustees were initially supportive of my actions and indeed because of my time-consuming efforts it had a positive effect and new members joined. However, later this did not continue. Maybe it might have been a power struggle thing, but I do not know the true reason. Quite frankly now, I don't much care.

Even though there was no argument, and it was trivial, I thought it best for all if I left.

Much later, I tried to re-join but surprisingly I was blocked. Irrespective of what happened in the past, which I consider to be of no significance, I still believe the concept of the group is good. Although, I do think the trustees are out of their depths at certain times they nevertheless can offer support and have contacts to assist injured officers in their fight against 'robust' Police Pension Authorities (PPA) who are reluctant to accept and award the correct IOD award.

I have made attempts to share the information of the campaign with the group by contacting current members. I know that the details of my campaign have been posted in their 'chat group' and discussed. I also know that a trustee posted a comment along the lines of, 'We need financial justice before a medal'. This coming from a trustee will have a degree of negative influence on many members, especially the vulnerable who are desperate for support at the worrying time of their battle to seek their correct injury award.

I believe the trustee(s) overlooked the rare opportunity to put their members plight in the spotlight and maybe get more attention. This could well lead to the wider broadcasting of the other bigger financial problem. What is certain is that by supporting the campaign, it cannot possibly do any harm. Not for the first time, I just cannot understand police based organisations shunning the proposal, especially when considering those it applies to.

Whilst I agree to a certain extent with the trustee's statement, in that finance is more important than medal recognition, the medal overlooking is an injustice too. It does not mean that the recognition should be totally ignored because of the widespread scandalous avoidance, often involving fraud and lack of any compassion, to save on budgets. As you read previously, I was a victim of this myself.

I do hope that all the members of IODPA hear of the campaign and decide to join in the support of it because many of them will be potential recipients.

On Tuesday, 28 November 2023, I found out that there was a National Police Federation, region 8, board member by the name of John Partington. Apparently one of his tasks is to act as coordinator for the pending posthumous medal, which IS supported by the Federation. I emailed him at 18.09 hours.

The following day, I found his mobile phone number, I rang it and to my surprise he answered. He appeared interested and patiently listened to my brief. I said that I would send him more information and I specifically requested that he acknowledge receipt of my email so that we would have confirmed connection, and he said that he would. He also said that he would be meeting with other board members the following week and he would discuss it with them.

Following on, I sent him two more emails, the second reminded him that he had not acknowledged or replied to my first. I asked if he would let me know the outcome of the discussion. I hoped for a reply by Friday 8 December, but I had heard nothing further from him at that time, including any acknowledgement. As difficult as it is, I tried to stay optimistic at least for the time being anyway. The significance of this contact is that it is the first time that I have actually been able to have direct contact with a member of the National Federation. All other dismissive contacts have come from mere county representatives.

On Friday 8 December ten days after our first contact I called his mobile number again, but it was after 4pm and there was no answer. I left a voice mail message requesting him to contact me. Up to that time I was not blaming the National Federation for not being onboard to support because for all I knew they might not even know about me or my campaign. My grievance was with the County Federation and as far as the National Federation was concerned my only complaint was the fact that they were not contactable.

On Tuesday, 12 December 2023, my patience and curiosity got the better of me and I again phoned John Partington. He answered the call, and a conversation took place as follows:

I said, "John, I'm disappointed that you did not, as agreed, reply to my three emails." He said, "Didn't I?" I said, "No, you didn't but have you spoken to the others?" He said, "Yes, but I haven't had anything back from them yet. I'm literally just about to get on a train. I will try and get back to you before I go on Christmas leave. I've had some personal problems and I need to look after myself." I said, "Of course you must, John but there are few things more important than our copper mates getting killed and maimed." He said, "The train's here now, I must go," and with that he was gone.

After the phone call ended, I got to thinking about what John had said. The first thing that entered my head was that of, '.... before I go on Christmas leave'. In 21 years of frontline uniform police service, I never once had a 'Christmas leave'. The most I got was either Christmas Day or Boxing Day off, but never did I have both off consecutively.

John's office can just simply closedown. John doesn't work Bank Holidays, nights, or weekends. He's got himself a soft 9 to 5 office job which does not involve him rolling about on the pavements wrestling with drunks when the clubs turn out at 2am, or some even later now.

The possibility of John and others in similar police office posts being injured I suggest is very unlikely. I wonder how long John had been on uniform patrol duties for? Nowhere near my 21 years I'll bet. He's nicely out of harm's way in his warm and safe office and where the majority of the time they do not take phone calls or reply to emails other than via the County Federations.

It was odd for him to share the, 'I've had some personal problems and I need to look after myself'. I think he'll be okay because he's shown he can 'look after himself' by securing a cushy little safe office number!

Well, even now when I'm 74, he can keep it because I joined the police to be a proactive police officer out on the streets with the public, not an office-bound clerk posing as one!

Maybe why I'm not gaining much interest for my campaign is because the ones I'm trying to get onboard have forgotten the dangers faced on the streets and have the 'I'm alright, pull the ladder up, Jack', mind-set!

I can't help feeling that John, knew for sure that he had not acknowledged my three emails. What was the, 'I've had personal problems' about? Was it no more than a feeble excuse and distraction?

It's hard to remain optimistic and see anything positive coming from John's involvement in light of that last conversation.

Is John about to get on a train or is it just a figment of his imagination? Is he merely trying to de-rail me? Have I hit the buffers with the Federation and is this the end of the track?

Tune in again for the next exciting episode of John and the run-away train... IF there is one!

Also on 12 December I received a very satisfactory response from an MP lobbied by my friend and former police inspector, Keith Ellis. The MP is Mr. Lloyd Russell-Moyle, Labour MP for Brighton, Kemptown. His email said that he'd written to Sir Roger Gale and Sally-Ann MPs and informed them that he fully supported my campaign and offered to help in any way he could.

Lloyd's email went on to say that he'd reached out to the 'National Police Federation' in response to his surprise that they were not also onboard and supporting. I had made his office aware of that and asked if Lloyd might make an approach because they were not listening to me, a 'nobody'! His obliging researcher, Tyler Poulter, had listened with interest and patience to my phone briefing, when he had rung me.

I must point out that Tyler had rung me as a response to my leaving a voice message on the office answer phone. During this campaign I can tell you that this response from an MP's office and especially when you are not one of their constituents is refreshing and an extremely rare occurrence. Most of the time, that does not happen even with my own MP's office for Sally-Ann Hart and that includes not replying to all my emails and I have had strong words with her staff about that.

Even being fully aware that I was not one of Lloyd's constituents, Tyler said that he believed he would agree to my request, and he was proven right in that belief.

So, I believed that this was an ideal opportunity to apply pressure on the National Police Federation. To build upon it, I instantly sent a request to Sir Roger and Sally-Ann to do the same as Lloyd Russell-Moyle. I figured that three contacts from separate MPs might be just the wake-up call the non-responsive Federation needed to kick-start them into action. To be honest, there is not much further action required from them because everything is in hand or already underway.

In my experience, any correspondence delivered with the House of Commons 'portcullis logo' on it always gets priority and best attention. I know from my police service, that envelopes bearing the logo always got opened first, with the combined emotions of apprehension and curiosity.

The only thing that may happen if the Federation do join us in support is they have the facility to circulate the campaign to all their serving officers. If that were to happen there may be an increase in petition signatures. Although, I wouldn't gamble on that given that NARPO circulated it to their 90,000 retired members and look at the depressing result from the so-called 'police family'. However, I must remain optimistic in the hope that numbers will increase significantly prior to the expiry date of the petition's life on 27 March 2024.

I sincerely value the willing support from Lloyd especially as he is a Labour Party MP and adds to our cross-party tally.

If I were Sir Roger or Sally-Ann, I'd be eager to duplicate Lloyd's approach to the Federation being that he is a Labour man, and they are both Conservatives. However, I believe the willing Sir Roger will oblige irrespective of anything other than my making a sensible and reasonable request.

It is so heart-warming to see cross-parties agree on something and make the rare offer to work alongside one another. To be a witness to that and not to see the so-called 'police family' do the same is deeply disillusioning and indeed disturbing!

Given the cross-party support being declared, I cannot honestly see this campaign failing.

As far as the Federation is concerned, I believe it is only a matter of time before they too throw their 'hat into the ring'. Irrespective of when that takes place, even now they are in a damage limitation zone for it has already gone past the time of, IF they end-up with egg on their faces but how much there will be!

I'm now left wondering if kindly Mr. Lloyd Russell-Moyle MP, may have just delivered the key to the Federation backdoor!

Forget the back door key, I reckon we're in!

On Friday 15 December 2023, I received a letter/email from Sir Roger Gale MP.

It reads:

Dear Tom,

Further to your email of the 12th of December I have in fact met, at a general meeting in the House of Commons with representatives of the Police Federation. I apprised them of my own initiative in this matter and they are not unsupportive but are concerned to ensure that the progress towards the Elizabeth Medal is not delayed. I think that is probably a matter that we can overcome.

With my best wishes.

Yours sincerely

Sir Roger Gale MP.

Well, well, well! Our 'Champion' Sir Roger, comes up trumps again, eh? I knew all the time during the dumb elusive antics of the Federation that at some time or another we would reach them.

I had emailed Sir Roger and told him of the Federation's shenanigans, and he must have immediately acted on my report.

I agree that my campaign should not delay the posthumous award proposal. However, it does worry me that when it is finally approved, without my proposal, what injured folks like poor Teresa Milburn will feel in being overlooked again. So, when the posthumous award is approved and the outcome finally announced, I do hope my proposal is fast tracked without delay towards approval. Once the posthumous award outcome is announced, we can maybe, with much haste, crack on with mine for the injured.

Hopefully, I can forget about the likes of John Partington, 'egg on their faces', Andy Standing, Daren Egan and the Federation more generally and concentrate on other concerns. The Federation are now irrelevant as the campaign is encouragingly progressing in the right direction i.e. to success. No doubt when that happens, they along with NARPO will try to pinch a bit of glory!

It's a great pity that the Federation did not tell me what they told Sir Roger but how could they because they obviously have no interest in listening to a 'nobody' so thank goodness we have a 'somebody' in our corner!

On Saturday 16 December 2023, I sent our MP Champion, Sir Roger this follow-up email:

Thank you for your last contact and for speaking with the elusive, to me, PFEW (Federation).

Sadly, for months they had no interest in speaking to me and my having been told by mere Sussex County Federation Representatives that they could 'not support it in its current form', albeit when asked what was 'wrong with the current form' they failed to reply, indicating that there was in fact nothing wrong with the 'current form' and only disinterest in thinking, what on earth could I, a nobody, have to say of any merit?

Sadly, such is the attitude in much of the world that that is why constituents are frequently forced in desperation to reach out to MPs knowing that the 'portcullis' heading will get best attention.

I totally agree that my campaign should not in any way impact on or delay that of the hopefully imminent, posthumous medal one.

However, it does cause me grave concern that on approval of the posthumous award it will cause upset to those injured and they will again be overlooked.

The best example is my much-referenced case of PCs Sharon Beshenivsky and Teresa Milburn who in 2005, in Bradford, were shot. Sadly, Sharon died but Teresa was saved.

When the posthumous award is approved and it's widely believed it will retrospectively be awarded, Sharon will undoubtedly be a recipient.

Teresa having survived will receive nothing and given they both attended the same incident, acted jointly and their actions were identical in every aspect, to overlook Teresa will be yet again a further snub. Teresa is likely not to be an isolated case.

On this occasion, I do not think the overlooking is deliberate but simply because no one else has thought of the repercussions on the injured.

The only way to avoid that unacceptable situation is to move as swiftly as possible on my proposal.

I believe I have previously referenced the Western Australia medal for those injured AND developed ill-health. See this link for further details:

https://en.wikipedia.org/wiki/Western_Australia_Police_Star

This is now a tried and tested award and confirmation that it would work in the UK. It also will cover those medically discharged with ill-health, who I confess I had not up to now given much thought to. They are also deserving given that they lost their job and thus were deprived of gaining the 'Long Service and Good Conduct Medal'. I believe they should be included in my proposal too.

Australia shares the same sovereign as the UK, I wonder if it might cause any less delay if we were to adopt the identical format. After all, by following their example we know it successfully works for them and so why would it not be the same for us?

I would kindly ask if you would give thought to my proposal and to pass the information of the above medal on to those you are in discussions with.

Kind regards

Tom Curry

I am hoping that based on the Western Australia medal, for those of their officers killed, injured or with ill-health, if similar were to be adopted here in the UK, then it might be a way to fast track it to approval.

On 18 December 2023, I have received this email from John Partington, National Federation:

John Partington—PFEW HQ

18/12/2023 09:18

Hi Tom

The view of the Federation is that in principle we would support such an award but would obviously need to see further details before we could commit further.

Regards

John

I emailed him all the relevant details and I await an acknowledgement.

On 20 December I received a message from Gordon Caldecott, my fellow administrator of our Facebook group. He said that he had emailed a Mr. Mark Jones, Secretary of the North Wales Federation and had received this reply:

Hi Gordon,

Yes mate, please pass on my contact details to your acquaintance. Probably best if he emails me all the details and then I will take it directly to the head of the Federation nationally to take this on. Having represented a number of officers who have been medically discharged it's absolutely right that they get the recognition.

He gave his mobile number and email address.

Refreshingly, this is the first time a Federation representative has ever willingly shown any real interest and supplied his mobile number and email address. I decided it would do no harm if Federation HQ had as many contacting them as possible to remind them that news of my campaign was spreading and was progressing. I emailed Mark the details straightaway, and I shall also phone him.

Mark replied to my email, and we spoke on the phone when I gave him my full brief. I am delighted that he said he will fully support the campaign proposal and will be broadcasting it to his serving members and to media contacts. He will also be contacting John Partington at the National Federation, and I believe this will encourage them to finally declare their full support and circulation to all UK serving police.

Mark is the first Federation representative who I truly felt grasped the importance of the campaign and was not merely going through the motions of expressing sincerity and compassion. He is a nice, genuine guy and I appreciate his support.

On 22 December I posted the following in our Facebook group:

Hi Guys,

My fellow admin. Gordon got in touch with his Federation Secretary of North Wales, Mark Jones and brought the campaign to his attention for the first time.

Mark welcomed the news and said for me to get in contact with him, which I did.

The result is that Mark fully supports the campaign on behalf of NW Federation and will be broadcasting the petition and Facebook group to his 1700 members. He will also do the same to other groups and media that he has access to. He has personally signed the petition and is a member of our group. He will be contacting John Partington at National Federation.

We really cannot expect any more from Mark, he being the first Federation man to appear enthusiastic about the campaign proposal and doing the right thing by his members.

I think this could be the start of the Federation finally getting their finger out and declaring their support, which I've always knew they will have to sooner rather than later.

Look at the farcical situation that is developing, National Federation is still not onboard, but NARPO is and now NW County is first to declare with Scotland teetering... others will follow, of that I'm confident.

We must not forget that my campaign and proposal was snubbed by Sussex Federation's Andy Standing (Sec.) and Daren Egan (Chairman). This blocked my getting to the National Federation and had a ripple effect when I tried the neighbouring Kent Federation and my own roots, Northumbria who followed suit and dismissed me too.

I'm hoping others will also contact their County Federation as Gordon did because it will help to add pressure.

Big thanks to Mark and our Gordon for his efforts and putting us in touch.

Tom

Mark's reply to my email:

Hi Tom,

It was really good to chat earlier and thank you for all the information in relation to your campaign. It is clear that a significant amount of work has already taken place and I just hope that I will be able to assist in progressing it even further for you.

I have already posted on our North Wales Police Federation Facebook page a link to the Government petition. Hopefully, others will start to see this, and the message will start to spread even further.

When the rest of the team are back in work in the New Year, which is only actually a couple of weeks away(!), then I will have a chat with them and see what else we can do.

As I said before, but will say it again, I am 100% behind your campaign and I know we will get there in the end.

Have a very Merry Christmas and all the best.

Mark Jones

Ysgrifennydd Cyffredinol a Thrysorydd | General Secretary & Treasurer

Ffederasiwn Heddlu Gogledd Cymru | North Wales Police Federation.

I have a feeling that good things will come about because of Mark's involvement. After all, as the adage goes - 'the greatest river starts with a trickle'.

However, I have had similar hopes dashed as in the case of David Kennedy of the Scottish Federation.

On 6 November 2023, he started off so well by declaring his support and promise of circulating it to his members and other contacts. It came to nothing and now once again my voice mails and emails remain unacknowledged.

This is the last email I sent on 22 December 2023:

Hi David,

North Wales Federation, Mark Jones has declared his full support and circulated it.

See the post on their FB site:

https://www.facebook.com/NWalesPoliceFed

John Partington National Federation who I'm in contact with, is teetering on declaring National Federation support.

I cleared the nonsense up re Bryn Hughes' non-existent move for the injured.

You could follow suit with NW Federation and circulate it to your members?

Your U-turn and hesitancy after you said you supported it is letting the campaign, the injured officers, your members and me down plus you went back to the non-replying to my contacts.

Kind regards

Tom Curry

On Wednesday 3 January 2024, I was prepared for the meeting with the Sussex Chief Constable Jo Shiner which was to take place the following day at 2.30pm OR so I thought!

However, at 5.30pm my phone rang, and it was Mr. Nellis. He was full of apologies for the late notice stating he'd just come back from leave, BUT the appointment with the CC was cancelled!

YEP, that's only 21 hours' notice and after months of waiting!

He said it was because, 'The team have sent it to the National Police Chief's Council (NPCC) as it is a national campaign and not confined to Sussex it would be inappropriate for the Chief to comment!' My first thought was 'What team?'

He said he thought, 'THE team had found out from media coverage'. I doubt that because it has only had a piece in Sussex News, 4 months past! I asked when did 'THE team send it to the NPCC? He said, 'He did not know but could try and find out'. I asked him to email me the full explanation and to find out when THE team sent it to the NPCC.

It does seem strange that the alleged 'well intentioned TEAM' did not bother speaking to me to gain knowledge of the up-to-date situation as to where the campaign is. They must think they either know it all, are clairvoyants or this 'nobody' is not worth speaking to. I fear decisions are likely to be made without them being in full possession of the facts and may even mislead the NPCC! After months of the Chief 'looking forward to hearing more when meeting me', she cancelled and in all that time she has done nothing in support.

According to Mr. Nellis 'THE team' appear to have not acted under the CC's instruction but of their own accord and have then advised her, surprisingly not the other way around.

There we go, I waited four months and with only 21 hours left prior to the meeting, the 'plug was pulled'.

I will have to remember to update the Sussex news reporter of this last-minute unexpected U-turn so he can include it when he does his follow-up article.

Yet further evidence in support of my book title, I submit! I await Mr. Nellis's email of explanation.

The following day, having had time to think over the previous day's surprising events I will now share my thoughts with you. There are things that I find difficult to understand and others I simply just do not believe.

I've already stated that because of the prolonged period it took to get an appointment to see the Chief Constable then that gives an indication as to how seriously the campaign and indeed myself are being taken. To inform me with 21 hours' notice and after 4 months waiting is totally unacceptable to such an extent it makes me want to swear but in the course of common decency, I will not subject you to that.

The Chief Constable will surely have known well before me being told that she no longer wished to meet with me. Paul Nellis used the excuse that he'd been 'on leave' but how long was his leave I ask? I see that as nothing more than a weak excuse.

To precis Mr Nellis's explanation, he said that, 'THE team had sent the details of the campaign to the NPCC, and they must have picked it up from the media'. I do not believe that, and I previously explained why. To accept that, one must believe that 'THE team' stumbled on my campaign only via Sussex News. They must have then ignored the tiny involvement, quote and photo of the Chief Constable and without consultation with the Chief Constable contacted the NPCC. She was then informed by THE team and decided it was 'inappropriate' to meet with me.

That simply does not add up and I would not be pleased if I were the

Chief Constable to hear of that behind-the-scenes involvement which I would view as undermining my position.

I truly believe the Chief Constable had second thoughts and ordered THE team, if such a thing exists, to contact the NPCC. If I'm right, then THE team will only have had scant details of the campaign, and certainly no more than the brief details given four months ago, on 15 September 2023, in the Sussex News. How were they ever going to give an accurate account to the NPCC without ever speaking to me, I am after-all leading the campaign?

For the Chief Constable to deem it 'inappropriate' to continue or comment purely because it dawned on her that it was a 'national campaign' is beyond the realms of the ridiculous. She knew it was a 'national campaign' when she gave the scant quote to the news reporter. If she did not then what did she think I was proposing, a medal just for Sussex officers? To expect that to be believed insults my intelligence.

It is now clearly apparent to me that the Chief Constable suddenly thought of self-preservation and opted to safeguard her own position above that of declaring full support for the campaign for the injured, many being her own officers.

Whist the compliant Mr. Nellis loyally tried to defend the Chief Constable by stating she did care and had only recently unveiled a memorial, I told him that type of deed was mere propaganda and did not demonstrate true care and sincerity. I compare that simple act with that of MPs appearing in public, shaking hands and kissing babies at election times. I need more than that example from the Chief Inspector to convince me of the Chief Constable's true feelings on the subject, especially after the sharp U-turn.

As far as it being 'inappropriate' to go ahead with the meeting and the lame excuse of avoiding involvement due to it being a 'national campaign', that is total rubbish. The one-to-one meeting could certainly have gone ahead, and the Chief Constable could have declared her PERSONAL support without seeking the backing of the NPCC. I see that action as having a lack of leadership and courage of your own convictions by first choosing the option of garnering the opinion of other equals prior to declaring where you personally stand, just to ensure your own profile is not harmed. I view it as being weak beyond belief and certainly shows the prioritisation of one's own position above that of expected care and decency to those less fortunate in my opinion.

Who with an ounce of human compassion would not instantly come out and say, 'I personally support this campaign to seek proper medal recognition for injured police officers'? For anyone, let alone a member of the so-called police family and especially a chief constable not to do so beggars belief. I submit that only the coldest of cold hearts would shy away from assisting this campaign.

SHAME on you Jo Shiner!

I just want to mention what I think of the Chief Constable's staff officer Chief Inspector Paul Nellis. We have had many lengthy conversations on the phone, and I believe him to be a polite and patient man. However, he is programmed to do the Chief Constable's bidding and indeed does so admirably, making good attempts to loyally defend her, whatever is put to him, even at the cost of the exact truth.

Although Paul has the diplomatic qualities for the job he does, I do not believe he is ever going to set the world on fire as a top cop. He may hold a senior rank, but he is no man hunter.

I joined the police to be on the streets and catch bad guys and I would choose that anytime above promotion and the role of an office-bound personal assistant. However, where he is now should go a long way towards his next promotion if he continues to do his mistress's bidding.

The likes of the Chief Constable and the Chief Inspector are relatively safe where they are and less likely to be injured than their frontline colleagues so they will view the need for my campaign differently.

As from this moment as far as I'm concerned, the Sussex Chief Constable is now irrelevant, and the campaign will simply continue. I am confident that she, along with the other ill-judged, will undoubtedly realise her mistake further on down the line and will then be eager to declare full support in the hope of claiming some credit.

I also view the Police Federation in the same way.

I intend very soon to give the go-ahead to Ms. Sally-Ann Hart MP to present my petition to the 'House.' However, for now, I will hold back on that for a short while in order to see if the Minister of State for Crime, Policing and Fire, Chris Philp, announces his decision after re-looking at my proposal, as requested by our Champion, Sir Roger Gale MP. I'll stick my neck out and say that I anticipate that will be favourable.

CHAPTER 8

CONCLUSION

When I first undertook the writing of this book, I initially decided that it would only be published at the end of the campaign, for fear of alienating some within police circles. If that were to prove to be the case, then my worry was that it might have had a negative impact on support.

However, what I could never have anticipated was the lack of support and disinterest of the majority with police connections. I have to admit that I was stunned by the overall reaction and indeed deeply disturbed by the 'couldn't care less' attitude from those you would expect more from. This is not merely isolated to the hierarchy within the Police Service, but it extends to the ordinary former lowest ranks of the retired.

To clarify as to whom I refer, I must point out that I have not been able to reach out to the current serving officers because my route to them has been barred by the Police Federation. There is no need to explain that statement any further because all has previously been revealed.

I can say that of the present serving police connections who I have encountered, the vast majority have disappointingly proven to be nonchalant as to my proposal. The odd one who has not been so, I have acknowledged in the book, but you will have seen that sadly that consists of no more than a handful. Certainly, where we are today with the campaign is no thanks to those connected to the Police Service.

It was suggested by certain parties at the beginning of January 2024, that I should publish the book as soon as possible instead of at the conclusion of the campaign. It was said that if the book were to be published during the campaign it might have the effect of bringing about more attention and it may also shock some into positively supporting the cause. I very much doubt that there will be the latter reaction, and in any case, I do not expect my book to be far-reaching.

However, I now realise that the book will have more purpose if circulated during rather than at the conclusion of the campaign. I have also come to believe that those who may be alienated are of no consequence because if they are not contributing anything whatsoever now there will be no detectable loss.

Having had it suggested to publish as soon as possible, I decided to pose the question to our Facebook group, 'Campaign for Medal Recognition for Injured UK Police Officers'.

Here is the link:

https://www.facebook.com/groups/1091080585216247

The overwhelming response from members was 'publish now' and that is what I will do.

I am slightly disappointed that the finality of the campaign will not be disclosed within the book. However, the benefits from publishing now vastly outweigh those of waiting. I want to make it absolutely crystal clear that the campaign has not in the tiniest way faltered. It is still going well, and all the signs are encouraging and as a matter of fact I am delighted with the progress. In this case it is MPs' support which is of paramount importance and not that of those within police circles.

I am confident, in consideration of the cross-party MP support that my proposal will be approved and when it is, undoubtedly it will be national news and thereby receive widespread media coverage. That being so, it will be highly unlikely that any interested party will go uninformed and besides throughout the duration of the campaign our Facebook group will exist, and updates will be available.

To all supporters, I offer my sincere thanks. To those affected injured officers, I assure you I will never abandon my campaign.

Stay safe

Tom Curry

Printed in Great Britain
by Amazon